Pickle Queen

The Life and Recipes of

Doris Jean Kay

Liz McCarty

54 Candles Publishing

Scottsdale, Arizona

Copyright © 2024 by Liz McCarty

Requests for permission to make copies of any part of the work should be submitted online at Liz@svTempest.com or mailed to the following address:

54 Candles Publishing Company
8369 N. Via Linda
Scottsdale, AZ 85258

www.54Candles.org

ISBN 978-0-9845545-5-3

No one has ever become poor from giving.

Anne Frank

We make a living by what we get. We make a life by what we give.

Winston Churchill

About this book …

When they're gone, their voices go silent. In the traditions of Mexico, a person lives on in immortality as long as her memory is kept alive. She dies only when forgotten. Doris Jean is gone, but she is remembered, not just by me, but by the countless people she touched with her kindness, caring and love. Yes, her voice has gone silent, but in this book, I will speak for her… in her own words. This is the story, complete with her recipes, of Doris Jean Kay. As you read it, you too may hear her laugh, see her smile, and feel her warmth.

I am Doris Jean Kay's oldest daughter. In 2018 and 2019, I interviewed my mother and recorded her life story. The interviews took place at various times in Show Low and Scottsdale, Arizona. The questions I asked evoked certain memories that were retold a few times during the process. I made the decision to include the recollections my mother repeated because it was her story and I assumed if she told something more than once, it must have been important to her.

The intent of interviewing my mother was to learn what I could about her life and the lives of those who impacted her. She was born and raised in a small community where almost everyone was related; in other words, one big family. I have several books about members of my family and really enjoyed reading them and learning about my ancestors.

My mother wasn't getting any younger and I didn't want to miss the opportunity to get answers to the questions I had. My father died in 2006 and I had regrets that I had not interviewed him. I was frequently reminded that when someone is gone, it's too late to ask that question.

At some point, I decided that I would also like to have a record of the food we ate as children. My sisters and I took on the task of going through my mother's recipes to add to this book.

This project would not have been possible without the input from my sisters. Victoria McCarty is a brilliant writer and helped add humor and humanity to the final product. Kathy Fish spent time proof reading both the book and the recipes that were included. A heartfelt thanks also go to Cathi Hull, Linda Anderson, and Mike Forde. Also, I must thank my husband of forty years, Howard Jones, for his help on all phases of this book.

I hope you feel the warmth.

Liz McCarty - 2024

Pickle Queen

Contents

Forward

In addition to being smack dab in the middle of the Great Depression, 1934 ushered in some of the most fearsome storms in the Dust Bowl. Bonnie Parker and Clyde Barrow died that year and J. Edgar Hoover became even more well-known when the FBI killed John Dillinger, Charles "Pretty Boy" Floyd, and Lester "Baby Face Nelson" Gillis. Alcatraz became a federal prison. Babe Ruth made his final appearance for the New York Yankees and Joe DiMaggio was purchased by the New York Yankees. What a year for the Yankees!

Music aficionados were enjoying Benny Goodman's "Moonglow" and Sons of the Pioneers' "Tumbling Tumbleweed." The top-grossing movie was *It Happened One Night* starring Clark Gable and Claudette Colbert. People were reading *Tender Is the Night* by F. Scott Fitzgerald and *The Postman Always Rings Twice* by James M. Cain.

Donald Duck made his first appearance in 1934. Pat Boone was born and Marie Curie died. A 14-pound pearl was found in the Philippines. A baseball cost 33 cents and a gallon of gas was ten cents. Franklin D. Roosevelt was president. Hitler, Mussolini, and Hirohito were already causing trouble. But at least there were cheeseburgers and Ritz Crackers. In late October of that year, another monumental event took place: the birth of Doris Jean Kay.

Yes, Doris Jean Kay came bopping into a small town in Arizona amidst an environment of poverty, dust, headlining gangsters, new discoveries and rumblings of war. It shaped who she was and how she lived. And she was feisty from the minute she got her first spanking by Dr. Heywood.

Chapter One

Roots and Branches

Taylor is a small town in northeastern Arizona settled by Mormons sent south from Salt Lake City by Brigham Young. Many of the residents were English, some with the distinction of crossing the plains in the first Mormon handcart company, desperate to leave England at a time when people were literally starving to death.

Snowflake lies just to the north of Taylor and the area has become famous around the state for its sweet corn. The growing season culminates with a Sweet Corn Festival on Labor Day weekend. However, the cash crop was not always sweet corn. During the 1940s and 1950s local farmers grew cucumbers for the Arnold Pickle and Olive Company. At that time the town celebrated by hosting a Cucumber Festival that started in 1948 and continued into the early 1960s.

Afton Kay

I was born on October 25, 1934, the youngest child of John Henry Kay and Eva Afton Hancock. My paternal great grandmother, Mary Ann Argyle, left Liverpool, England on March 22, 1856, on the sailing vessel Enoch Train. She was barely ten years old.

My grandparents on both sides were born in Taylor. Yet, I know very little about the Hancocks, including where they were before arriving in Taylor.

My earliest recollections of older family members were my maternal grandparents, William Hancock and Eva Lewis. My Grandfather Hancock was a special man and I thought the world of him. He wasn't at home a lot, but when he was, he wanted to help my widowed mother and her four children. I remember him coming to the house and splitting wood for our family's only source of heat, an old wood-burning stove.

Eva Lewis and William Hancock

Granddad Hancock worked out of town most of the year as he was employed by one of the Basque sheep ranchers in the Mesa area. He brought their sheep to the White Mountains to graze each summer and headed back to Chandler in the fall. When he was in town, he usually had the pack mules used for his work. He let me and my sisters ride the mules. What great fun for a young girl! My sisters and I played in the barn and helped in my grandparents' beautiful yard.

My grandmother Hancock was a severe, quiet little lady who was short and a little bit chubby. Often, she was very sharp and she was not a happy person. When we Kay girls went to visit, it was hard to be around her since she was quite ornery.

William and Eva Hancock were hard-working, church-going people. They looked after my sisters and me, sometimes attending school or church events in which we were involved. In the small town of Taylor, life revolved around church and Sunday school, which provided the only legitimate activities for the townspeople.

I loved my grandfather Hancock. At times, he met me at the school bus stop and walked home with me. He told me I had some of his characteristics and that I would make a good sheepherder because I could walk as fast as he could, which came in handy when I hiked with my own children. He was a fast walker. When we got to the house, he split wood and I hauled it to the side of the house.

My Grandma Hancock was a good person, if one defined that as faithfully attending her church meetings. In reality, she was judgmental and mean and I hope those are not inheritable traits. Grandma Hancock was not a person I liked and I could never seem to get close to her.

There was a sense that Grandma Hancock was cruel to my mother because my mother was pregnant when she married my father. In fact, my mother's sister, Emily, also ended up on the list of persons out of favor because she married John Baldwin against my grandmother's wishes. After the marriage, Emily was not very happy but Grandma Hancock told her she "had made her bed and now had to lie in it". So at least two of Grandma Hancock's children were not at the top of the Christmas list.

Another demonstration of my Grandma Hancock's testiness was one Halloween when my sister Corrine dressed up like Aunt Jemima. When we arrived at Grandma Hancock's home and she answered the door, Corrine announced "Well, Grandma, I'm as fat as you are now." As one can imagine, this did not endear

Corrine to Grandma and another name dropped from the Christmas list.

My oldest sister, Louise, began dating a local boy, Jay Hatch. When they announced their wedding plans Grandma Hancock was not a happy camper. She wrote Louise a nasty letter informing her that her kids were going to be idiots because Louise and Jay were third cousins. Louise was a kind and sensitive young woman and this really hurt her feelings. Grandma was different than Louise to say the least.

The Hancock's were religious and to my knowledge believed all of the teachings of the Mormon Church. They were sealed in the LDS Temple and welcomed ten children into their family. Two died in infancy. I always suspected that Eva resented the fact that William had to work out of town most of the time, which left her with the task of caring for their large family. Grandma was a homemaker and (to my knowledge) never worked outside the home.

Grandma Hancock had a small garden and some grapevines. She was an avid quilter and sewed the family's clothing. Granddad was a sheepherder his entire working life, although periodically he met the train in Holbrook and took the freight on a wagon to Whiteriver.

I enjoyed my Hancock grandparents and knew they were always there if I needed anything although they didn't help as much as the Kay relatives. After the children were grown and married, Grandma joined Granddad in Mesa each winter. In fact, they celebrated their fiftieth wedding anniversary in Mesa.

I spent more time with my grandmother Kay than I did with my grandmother Hancock and even as a young girl, I suspected there was some jealousy. When I was in high school the bus stopped in front of Grandma Hancock's house, but I went straight to Grandma Kay's home without stopping to say hello. Grandma Hancock expressed displeasure. But I ignored her.

We were closer with the Hancock side of the family as a whole because they were good about having reunions. The reunions allowed us to get to know our extended Hancock family. The Kays never had reunions.

I remember going to my Hancock grandparent's home for Thanksgiving one year just before they left for Chandler for the winter. We had turkey, giblet gravy, sweet potatoes and green beans she had canned from her garden. This meal is memorable to me because Grandma Hancock was not the best cook and the giblet gravy was especially good. Maybe my mom made it.

I loved my Grandfather Hancock dearly. I remember vividly one lesson I inadvertently learned from him one day. An Ellsworth from Show Low came walking by the house. He was drunk, and addressing my grandfather, he said "Hi, Will. Could you loan me ten dollars?" My grandfather's response was, "I loaned you ten dollars once and you never paid me back. I'm not loaning you another nickel." My grandfather Hancock was the only father-figure I had and I always remembered that encounter.

For years my grandfather walked from Chandler to Sheep's Crossing with the Basque sheepherders. They had a place in Heber where my uncle Byde, my mother's brother, stayed each summer. One summer Corrine earned money by staying in Heber with Uncle Byde to do the cooking and cleaning. I think it was only a small shack.

Rebecca Standifird, my father's mother, was born in Utah and came to Taylor as a small child. Shortly after the family arrived in Taylor, Rebecca's father decided to comply with the LDS church's mandate to take a second wife. He announced that he planned to marry his wife's sister. Rebecca's mother, Mary Ann Argyle, did not welcome this news. She moved out of the house promptly. And she (and her children) moved into a cave in Shumway.

I don't know where my Grandfather Kay was born. His family was from Lakeside. He died in 1918, a victim of the Spanish flu epidemic. He served in World War I and I don't know if he contracted the flu in Europe or upon his return to Taylor. My grandmother raised their seven children by herself. She supported them by running the bunkhouse in Standard, a sawmill town southeast of Taylor. My dad worked at the saw mill. My mother, who was known as Afton, helped her mother-in-law cook at the bunkhouse. She gleaned her marvelous cooking skills by working at the bunkhouse with my Grandma Kay.

Rebecca Standifird was a member of the Church of Jesus Christ of Latter-day Saints, as were the majority of Taylor residents, then and now. She, too, had been sealed in the LDS Temple. Sealing meant that you would be with your earthly family for all eternity. Yet my memories of my Grandmother Kay are in stark contrast to my Grandmother Hancock.

Grandma Kay was so much fun. She took my sisters and me swimming in the Silver Creek in Shumway, stripping down to her temple garments. This made her the talk of the town. Grandma Kay could cuss a blue streak and she was an excellent cook. Always welcoming, she often hosted large family dinners. The only time I can recall a big dinner with the Hancock's was one Thanksgiving.

The cellar under Grandma Kay's home was always full of canned meat, tomatoes, peas, corn and plum jam. Whatever she grew in her garden was preserved for long winters. The garden was located on the east portion of her large property along with plum trees.

There was a barn on the property and Grandma had a cow and chickens. She could ring the neck of a chicken in no time flat. A mean rooster ruled the grounds and he didn't like my sister, Louise. Whenever she came around, he ran after her and jumped on her. Had he remembered my Grandma Kay's skill at killing chickens, perhaps he might have been a bit more cautious. Grandma helped my mother as much as she could with food. She always had sugar cookies or doughnuts to offer her grandchildren. She was a very good cook and a hard worker.

Grandma Kay was kind and hard working. She would have given the shirt off her back to anyone. I remember her as kind, considerate and generous. I attribute my work ethic and my love of cooking and gardening to my grandmother Kay. If I am in any way a generous person, I attribute that to her as well.

Rebecca was raised as a Latter-day Saint and went to church every Sunday. She wanted her granddaughters to attend church weekly as well. I loved my grandmother very much. My grandparents were very good people and they were very caring and kind.

Both my mother's and father's families were extremely religious. Most activities centered on the Mormon Church. There was really nothing else to do in such a small town where almost everyone was Mormon. My mother didn't attend church very often when I was growing up as she had to work most Sundays.

Our family spent lots of time at Grandma Kay's house. We had many dinners there and I remember Uncle Floyd was there a lot. My sisters and I didn't like him. He was married to my dad's sister, Irene. He was so obnoxious. He'd pull our underwear down. He was there all the time. Once when we went to visit and he was there, my sister Janice disappeared. We searched and searched for her and finally found her, locked away in a tiny closet. She had wanted desperately to hide from Uncle Floyd. I don't think he abused her, but he embarrassed her because of the things he did. I remember my sisters and I walked to the store to buy groceries for my mother. If we happened to see Uncle Floyd driving by, we'd dive into the bushes on the side of the road to hide from him.

When we were quite young, my father's sister, Aunt Fanny, and her family moved to Bonners Ferry, Idaho. She was never able to return and I don't think Grandma Kay was ever able to travel to Idaho to visit. I don't know what Fanny's husband did for a living so I don't know what took them to Bonners Ferry.

I was born in my Hancock grandparent's two-story home in Taylor, Arizona. I lived in the same house for my entire childhood and left only after I married. The house had once belonged to the Warners. Mrs. Warner died and in the later years my grandmother Kay married Joe Warner. We referred to him as Uncle Joe.

My mother's little sister, Doris, died in infancy. I was named after her and have no idea where my middle name, Jean, came from. I am the youngest of four girls. I know my mother loved me because she told me all the time. I went to grade school in Taylor and high school in Snowflake.

My childhood home was little and consisted of just two rooms. The kitchen housed a table, a wood burning cook stove, a box for the wood for the stove and a washstand. Since the house had no running water, we filled the tin basin on the washstand with water from our well.

The main room contained two beds, a few chairs and a dresser with very little in it. We only had the bare necessities. The kitchen held a small closet, but it didn't need to be any bigger because we just didn't have very much. We also had an outhouse and an old tin bathtub. We filled the bathtub with water we heated on the cook stove. We bathed inside and when we emptied the tub after bathing, we hung it outside on the house on a nail.

We had a small cellar that held our canned goods. I hated to go into the cellar. It gave me the creeps. I was certain it was full of spiders even if I couldn't see them. It kept things nice and cool. After I married Witt, he and Paul Patzke, a contractor friend, installed a new kitchen in my mother's mobile home. While doing the work, he found an old crock sitting on a rock near the entrance to that old cellar. I asked my mother if I could have it. She gave it to me. I didn't get very much from her, but I did get that old crock. It had belonged to my Hancock grandparents. They made pickles in it.

My earliest memories are of running around Taylor all the time. We had the creek east of the house and we played outside a lot. I was a tomboy and loved to climb trees from a very young age. There were mulberry trees on the Standifird property.

My family was very poor because my father died when I was four. My mother worked but didn't make very much money. She did receive a small amount of money from the Industrial Commission after my father died, but the attorney took most of that. She received $60 per month until I turned eighteen. I don't know how my mother paid for my hospital bill when I had to have my appendectomy. She didn't talk about money much, but when she needed some and didn't have it, we all knew it.

Louise was the oldest of my sisters so the task of caring for us while my mother worked fell on her shoulders. She made sure we did our chores around the house and in the garden. I didn't resent her for doing her job. However, Corrine was another story. She was pretty hard-headed and wouldn't help out unless she was forced. Janice was probably most like me. We pretty much did what we were told.

Janice, Louise, and Doris Kay

I fought with Corrine all the time. She picked on me constantly and was always beating me up. When I was a freshman in high school, there came a reckoning. I was fed up with her being so mean to me. I was not going to take it anymore. One day I cornered her on the bed and beat the crap out of her. After that she left me alone.

I got along well with Janice. We were closer in age and did many things together. She let me run around with her and her friends. One time when I wasn't with them, they stole a bunch of turkeys and chickens. They brought them to our house and cooked them making a huge mess. My mother was furious and made them spend the next day cleaning up the house. They never did that again.

We definitely got into some trouble from time-to-time. But really, for four girls, we got along pretty well when we were together.

We had lots of things that had been planted on our property. We had green and blue gage plums, gooseberries and currants. The currants were the black currants and they were so good. My mother made pies out of them. We canned the gooseberries every year and she made gooseberry pie. We had to help with a lot of the picking of the berries. We didn't mind because that was the food we had in the winter. Asparagus grew along the banks of the ditch that ran by the house and my mother would go out and cut it when it was nice and tender so we had that to eat in the spring.

We picked cucumbers in the summer for twenty-five cents a lug. It took at least four hours to pick a lug. We had to lift each vine and search for the cucumbers and the vines were mean. They protected themselves with sharp stickers. You had to be a good picker or they didn't want you back in the field. If you weren't a good picker, they ended up with big cucumbers that nobody wanted. I was a good picker. My mother let us keep the money we earned.

My childhood was very happy. We spent a lot of time in the creek below the house. We went swimming and wading and chasing pollywogs. In the front yard we had a ditch with a rickety old bridge across it. Lots of times we could see muskrats in the water going back and forth. Sometimes we went out to the pavilion with these crummy skates we owned and skate for hours. Reed Hatch, my dad's cousin, built a swimming pool for the town that was near the town well. It was kept full in the summer and was icy cold. I think we paid ten cents to swim all day. But we would sneak in there at night and go swimming in our underwear.

I was a tomboy and a momma's girl. Everyone said I was spoiled, but I wasn't nearly as spoiled as Janice. She was ill most of the time and my mother had to spend a lot of time with her. I don't remember what happened, but one time she lost all of her hair. Her hair wasn't as thick as the rest of us after that.

Corrine, on the other hand, was always in trouble. I don't know why. It was one thing after another. She was a wild one. Once my mother took a stick to her because she wouldn't help with the chores. Corrine taunted my mother saying it didn't hurt. After that my mother said she would never touch Corrine again and she didn't. I don't remember my mother ever spanking me, but I'm sure she did because I was no angel.

We helped Grandma Kay a lot. We picked lots of things from her garden so she could bottle them. We had fresh peaches every year, but from where they came, I can't remember. I know they grew them in Whiteriver and maybe that's where we got them.

We used to drive to Lone Pine Dam in Uncle Joe's old pickup and go 'graping.' We picked the wild grapes and made jam, something I also did with my own daughters. We made plum jam too, but it wasn't my favorite. We grew and preserved our own food or we didn't eat, like many others.

In the summer, Grandad Hancock drove the sheep from Chandler over the Superstition Mountains through Heber to Sheep's Crossing in the White Mountains. Sometimes, he brought us a leg of lamb and sometimes some trout he caught at Sheep's Crossing. He packed them in watercress to keep them cool until he got to Taylor. The trout were cleaned and we fried them. They were so small that the bones dissolved. They were really good.

I didn't and still don't care for lamb, perhaps because we ate so much of it. My mother didn't make lamb stew, she roasted it instead. Sometimes she cut it into small pieces and fried it. My mother's sister, Leah, made lamb stew all of the time and I just couldn't stomach it. My mother loved lamb. Later in her life, on the way back from visiting Corrine in New Mexico, we went through Zuni. My mother asked to stop at a trading post so she could buy lamb. She was disappointed because they didn't have any.

We always made it a point to clean and decorate our relatives' graves on Memorial Day. Fern Standifird, my dad's cousin, taught us how to make our own flowers to decorate the graves after we cleaned them. We purchased multiple colors of crepe paper. Fern had patterns and we traced them. We ended up with a thick stack, as many as we could cut. We made the flowers, put a wire around a bouquet to hold it together and covered the wire with green crepe paper. They made a 16" by 16" box with a piece of glass for the cover. We put the flowers in the box and placed the boxes on the graves. We spent hours and hours making the flowers and the boxes. Sometimes we took the time to dip the flowers in wax. We didn't have any money so that's the only way we had something for the graves every year. That's why I still like to decorate them every Memorial Day.

We spent lots of time at the Standifird house. We even referred to Fern as our second mother. She had no children and couldn't go anywhere because she was so crippled from being run over by a wagon. We went there and talked with her. She played the piano and we all sang along.

I also grew up with the Hatches because my mother worked for Burt Hatch at The Grill. We played canasta and made tacos. Grace Hatch was the 4-H teacher and she taught me a lot about sewing.

My dad died when I was only four years old. I remember the body being in the house for one or two nights. I did not like it, but that was the custom. The morning he was buried my mother was so distraught she wanted to jump in the grave. Left alone with four little girls ranging in age from four to ten was almost more than she could bear.

The only source of ice for our family was in winter when icicles formed on a waterfall just south of our home. My sisters and I broke them off and made ice cream. We shared it at get-togethers. My mother's sister, Leah, was married to my father's cousin Speed Standifird. That meant family gatherings were usually comprised of both sides, including Leah, Speed, Fern and Uncle Quill, Fern and Speed's father.

Fern Standifird (center)

Chapter Two

Small Town Charm

It was much colder in Taylor in the 1930s and 1940s so when my mother had a side of beef, she hung it out on the north side of the house. When she was ready to cook, she had to haul the beef into the house and saw off enough for a meal.

We had a cow, but it wandered out into the road one day and was hit and killed by Arlee Maxwell, a man we knew from Show Low who worked for the Arizona Department of Transportation. After that we had to buy milk from a neighbor. This is the reason I don't like milk to this day. It had the bluish tint that is raw milk with the cream floating on top. But the real problem was the smell of the neighbor's house. It reeked of milk and babies.

My sisters all took piano lessons and sang. Janice had a really good voice and the four of us sang together. They used to have what they called "soldier parties" at the church for men going to war. We were usually invited to sing at those parties. They introduced us as The Kay Sisters.

World War II loomed huge in my younger years. It was a scary time for me. My uncles Dick, Byde and Ferris Hancock all joined the service. The Standifird boys joined as well but two didn't return. I don't know what their jobs were, but they flew together and their plane disappeared. To this day, each time I see something on the news about finding an old plane it brings back memories and I wonder if they will finally find them. Speed is the only one that returned home after the war.

My best friend was Margie Reidhead. She was so much fun. I ran around a lot with Louise McCleve and Barbara and Sharlene

Hatch. My mother worked for their dad so we did a lot of things together.

There was a movie theater in Snowflake and if I wanted to go, I had to find a ride. The talk of the town was *Gone with the Wind* because Clark Gable cussed. I don't remember when I first saw that movie, but I did see it again in the late '70s or early '80s in Scottsdale with Joe Blair, when we were dating. I really didn't have much of a chance to see any movies because of my family's financial condition.

I was required to attend church all the time and of course there was Mutual, a weekly night of wholesome activities for the youth of the Mormon Church. I learned to square dance and to round dance at Mutual. We had a dance once a month. The music was produced by a phonograph.

I didn't even see a television until after I had been married for quite some time. We had a big radio and, in the summer while my mother was working, we listened to country music on KKOB from Albuquerque. During the war, when President Roosevelt was going to speak, my mother gathered us around the radio to listen. We couldn't make a sound because she wanted to hear every word he said.

We had a cat named Coo and a white cat that was really Janice's. I don't remember its name but it loved popcorn and so did Janice. Janice would start a batch of popcorn and the white cat's eyes would start running. That cat could eat more popcorn than any of us. We loved our cats and dressed them up in doll clothes. We used to catch toads and dress them up as well.

We had a dog once, but my mother got rid of him because he wouldn't quit tearing our clothes off the clothesline. Clothing was in short supply so we didn't even have him long enough to give him a name.

When I wanted to be alone, I climbed a mulberry tree and sat there quietly. Sometimes I hid in the grass near the plum bushes that were at the end of the Standifird property. One time Corrine and some of her friends killed a porcupine and roasted it near the plum bushes so I never went back. They said they ate the porcupine. Maybe they did. But I didn't want to try it.

I was always hungry and home alone, so I learned to cook when I was quite young. We had canned fruit and my mother taught me to make pie crust so I could make a pie. One time, Corrine and I made a tuna mixture. We didn't have a refrigerator or icebox so it went bad and both of us got food poisoning.

I remember a terrible summer storm one time when we were all home alone. The wind was blowing really hard and our roof started leaking. I told Corrine that we might as well be sitting out in the rain because we were getting so wet inside the house. Corrine laughed about that for years.

I daydreamed about having a nice house someday. All of us dreamed about that. We didn't have much of a house but we were happy. Really, most people in Taylor didn't have very much. I was thrilled when Louise and Jay and Jim and I could afford to add a bedroom and bathroom onto my mother's house. Later, the four of us bought her a mobile home and life was much better for her.

Our neighbors, the Harrison's, moved to Taylor from Arkansas. One day Mrs. Harrison dropped by the house and gave us some black-eyed peas. We had never seen black-eyed peas and didn't know what to do with them. They were still in a pod in a paper bag. Even my mother didn't know what to do with them. A few days later Mrs. Harrison dropped by again and wanted to know if we had cooked them. When I told her we hadn't, she asked to have them back so I gave them to her.

I loved my mother's beans and homemade bread. Sometimes, if my mother was home for a few days, she made a pink pudding. I assume it was packaged strawberry pudding and I loved it. She also made such good pies that I didn't have a favorite. We ate the pies with homemade ice cream. I had a lot of favorite dishes.

Mom made wonderful macaroni and cheese. Her fried potatoes were so crispy and good. I loved her fried rabbit and potatoes and gravy. Her cinnamon rolls were excellent. I can still smell them. She had to cook them in the wood stove so they had caramel on the bottoms. She always put raisins in them and that's how I love them to this day.

We didn't have enough money to have birthday presents, but I do remember my mother trying to make a cake for me several times. Cakes were not her strength. They always fell. She tried but they were never very good. I always remember my birthdays as family events spent with the Standifirds.

At the end of each summer my granddad Hancock headed back to Chandler from Sheep's Crossing with the sheep. His route took him through Taylor. My sisters and our Hancock cousins were always excited to see him with the pack mules. Riding them was such fun. But one year when Corrine, Janice and I waited with our cousin, Bill Baldwin for our turn to ride, I chose a wild, wild mule. I couldn't do a thing to control him and was lucky to dismount without breaking my neck. One ride that summer was enough for me.

The LDS church was a huge influence on my sisters and me. My mother was not as religious as most people, but she tried to make sure we attended Sunday school. As a child I attended Primary, religious instruction for Mormon children, and memorized all the things they gave us. My family blessed our food and said our prayers at night before we went to bed. I was forced to take religious education classes called Seminary in high school. Church functions were a big part of our social life. That was the only place to do anything. We learned to dance and all our activities were done in association with the LDS church. There were only two families in town that didn't belong to the LDS church, the Kizzars and the Harrisons. Eventually the Harrison children joined the church and the Kizzars moved to Clay Springs.

We celebrated Easter and Christmas, but I didn't realize they were religious holidays. I just thought it was a time to get together with family for big dinners and picnics.

When I was a child, people were quarantined for typhoid fever. If someone brought food to the home of someone that had been quarantined, they had to leave it outside for the sick family. One time a rabid dog decided to make our backyard his home. We had to stay inside until someone came to kill it. I was very frightened.

One of my happiest memories was being able to spend time in Winslow for a few weeks in the summer. Aunt Stella, my mother's sister, had a daughter, Anna Lou, who was a year younger than Janice and a year older than me. I just couldn't believe my good fortune. It was such a change and I really looked forward to it. Winslow was the big city (population 4,000) and Aunt Stella had lots of plans. We got to shop at the doll store and we were allowed to walk around town all by ourselves. My uncle worked for the railroad, so we spent time at La Posada, a beautiful hotel where the train stopped, watching the trains come and go.

Anna Lou had three younger brothers. We weren't used to being around boys and I thought these particular boys behaved like monkeys. Bobby, Billie and Jerry rose at the crack of dawn just so they could torment us by climbing on everything in the bedroom. Years later, Billie joined the Air Force. On his way home from Guam, he was killed in a plane crash.

I had the usual childhood diseases, mumps, measles, chickenpox and whopping cough. I had stomach problems for years and no one could figure out what was wrong with me. While on my visit to Winslow the summer after my freshman year, I got really sick. My aunt took me to see Dr. Wright and I had to have my appendix removed. The time I spent in the hospital along with having to take it easy for months completely ruined my summer.

When I was in the eighth grade, Dr. Haywood extracted my tonsils and I was sure I was going to die. He shook like crazy and sent me home shortly after the surgery. I couldn't stop bleeding. Uncle Quill said he had something to stop it and stuck a powdery substance down my throat. I don't know what it was, but the bleeding stopped immediately.

Even though I was quite the tomboy, I only suffered a few scraped knees and elbows. As far as the rest of the family was concerned, Corrine fell in the ditch when she was little. They found her because her bonnet caught on something. They were able to revive her. She got sick once and her hair fell out and when it grew back, it was curly. Both Corrine and Janice might have had the measles and that caused their hair to fall out. Vaccines for measles and mumps were not available when we were kids.

Grandma Kay let us keep our cow in her barn and the barn had a hay loft. Janice and I accompanied my mother one night for the milking so we could play in the hay loft. Somehow, Janice lost her balance and fell, catching her leg on a nail on the way down. Her flesh was hanging out. My mother had to take care of it herself. Janice was in a lot of pain and the scrape left a huge scar.

My mother was so very kind to me and my sisters, but she was also strict. Life in the waning years of the Great Depression was hard. She was giving it everything she had, but her four girls had to help. She taught us how to split wood, carry it to the house and build fires, clean, cook, help with the laundry, ironing, washing and drying the dishes along with pulling weeds and working in the garden. We used a wood cook stove for cooking and the only heat in the house was wood.

We had to do our laundry every Saturday and on top of that we had to make the soap. My mother taught us how to do this. She had a big black kettle outside and into it went lye and other ingredients. We had to pour it into a big tray to let it harden and then cut it into bars so we could use it to do the laundry. We used the same black kettle to do the laundry. We started with the whites. We boiled the water and stirred it constantly with a stick. The whites had to be rinsed twice and then we added a bluing solution to insure the whitest clothes in town. There was no dryer so everything had to be hung out to dry. Mom insisted that everything be ironed, including the bras and panties.

Laundry was done outside no matter the weather. We hoped for a wind so that the clothes would dry faster and not just freeze to the line. This explained why everything had to be ironed.

On Saturday after the laundry was hung out to dry, we had to clean the kitchen from top to bottom. We had a little cupboard with curtains across the top. That cupboard had to be emptied and scrubbed each and every Saturday. We scrubbed the kitchen floor on our hands and knees with a brush using the water that was discarded from the white laundry. That old pine floor was bleached white from the cleanings we gave it.

We had to wash the bed sheets weekly and just hope they dried in time for bed that night. Once someone gave us a dog. Can you imagine giving us a dog when we could hardly feed ourselves let alone one more little mouth? The first week we had the dog the sheets were blowing in the wind and he decided to tear the sheets off the line. Guess how long we had that dog? It was gone the very next day! I don't know what happened to it, but it was gone.

Our family was close and we laughed a lot. Christmas was a special time. Each of us got new robes and a stocking. There was a fresh orange in the toe and the rest was filled with nuts and hard candy. There was also a little toy in each. My dad died in November and the year he died Burt Hatch's family gave each of us girls a doll. If we didn't eat Christmas dinner at home, we went to my grandmother Kay's. I don't remember eating Christmas dinner with my Hancock grandparents.

I don't remember my mother sitting around very much when we were growing up. She had to cook every meal on a wood stove that required lots of cleaning in order to use. The chimney had to be cleaned. We spent Saturday doing laundry and, in the evening,

Mom cooked lots of fried potatoes and macaroni. That was all we had because money was tight. There was very little meat in the summer because there was no way to keep it from spoiling.

My mother let us have cats, but they weren't allowed in the house. They were outdoor cats and if they had kittens, she usually put them in a gunny sack and drowned them in the ditch because she didn't want them. Only years later did I realize why she did that. There was no way to spay the cat and we had cats running out our ears. I remember we had a big calico cat named Coo. I have no idea who gave her that name, but she got stung by a bee. The poor thing was rolling around crying.

My mother went to work at The Grill Café for Uncle Wren, my father's brother. Several years later, Wren sold the cafe to Burt Hatch. Uncle Wren went down the street and opened a place called Kay's Confectionery. My mother continued to work at The Grill. She was the cook and made all of the pies. The menu consisted of beef stew, oyster stew, hamburgers and Coney Island hotdogs. There was beer for drinking on the premises as well as packaged liquor to go. The Grill Café is where I met my first husband, Jim McCarty.

One thing that really stands out to me about The Grill is that they wouldn't let black people in the door. They had a little window where they came and placed their orders. We made it and handed it out to them at that window. They were not allowed inside. At that time, no blacks lived in Snowflake or Taylor. They traveled between Holbrook and McNary and stopped to eat at The Grill on their travels. I always felt that the people who lived in my little town were judgmental about color and people. I suppose this means that they were bigots and racists.

What did my mother do for fun? Not a lot as she had four kids that she was trying to raise by herself. However, sometimes my uncles came by and I dreaded it. Uncle Glen Baldwin who was married to my mother's sister, Emily, and Uncle Dick Kay, my dad's brother drank a lot. Especially Uncle Dick and he could be just sloppy drunk. Sometimes my mom and Speed and Leah went to Show Low to the Blue Moon to go dancing. This seldom happened as she had to work so much. She wasn't able to go to church with us so we just went by ourselves.

Leah and Jack (Speed) Standifird

Our heat for a long time was a fireplace and it wasn't that good. In fact, it almost set the house on fire. One day it was burning and Corrine and I went outside and realized that it had burned a hole through the chimney and was about to catch the house on fire. We managed to get the fire out and Uncle Speed patched the hole. Then they installed a wood-burning Ashley stove making it a lot warmer and nicer in the house.

I have a southern accent from my mother's side of the family. My mother and her mother both had this same southern drawl. I believe the Hancocks came to Taylor from Missouri, but people always think I am from Georgia. I tell them I am from south

Taylor. I am built like my mother as well. I'm tall and thin with thin legs. My head is small like hers and of the same shape.

I hope I am as kind and thoughtful as my mother was. She did not have a lot of time to help other people because she worked so hard to take care of us. I've had more chances to help others. My mother was organized and hard-working. She was clean and I have realized over the years how much it meant to me to live in a clean house and to be organized. She was a good person. She was brought up by her parents to be good and kind.

Doris Kay McCarty and Afton Kay

My mother worked hard because she wanted us to have an education and to finish high school. Louise got married when she was 16 and dropped out of school. Corrine dropped out as well.

She was so ornery she was going to do things her own way no matter what. Both of them completed their junior year in high school, but neither ever went back to finish school or get a GED. My mother made sure we finished our homework each night. It was very important to her that we finish school. She worked hard to be a good mother because we had no one else.

We had a cow (until it wandered onto the highway), rabbits and a pig. We had to take care of those animals because they were our source of food.

Every year for my birthday my mother fried a rabbit. It was my favorite dish along with mashed potatoes and gravy, which we seldom got. Sometimes, my Grandma Kay gave me a huge bouquet of chrysanthemums. She grew them on the north side of her house and they always bloomed on my birthday.

When I turned eight, I was baptized into the LDS church. It was late October and the baptism took place in the creek below our house. It was icy cold and I was scared to death; but I lived through the great submerging.

I will never forget one time when Louise and Corrine got in trouble. Grandma Kay had a beautiful garden with all of these peas just ready to pick. She had planned that the next morning she would pick and can all of them. Corrine, Louise and a couple of cousins beat her to the picking and ate every last pea raw. When my mother found out she grabbed a stick and began to chase them. They were able to outrun her only because she fell down on the road in front of the house. Her knees were a bloody mess and it took weeks for them to heal properly.

My mother was the biggest influence on me during my younger years. She impressed upon me to be honest, hard-working and clean. Another big influence was my granddad Hancock. He was so hard-working and a good person. I loved him dearly.

My sister, Louise, was six years older than me and she was in charge when my mother was working. I watched her and followed lots of things she did. She had to learn by the school of hard knocks and she taught me what she learned.

I will never forget my Grandmother Kay. She was a special lady and had so much fun. She believed in the gospel but never preached to us. Being around her made me feel like a good person. I always felt so close to her. There was no doubt that she was the favorite of my sisters as well. We learned to work spending time with Grandma Kay and she made work seem like fun.

Aunt Leah was another big influence. She babysat us many times when my mother needed help. When I was a child, Leah's husband drowned near Bullhead City. I believe he had gone fishing with his two brothers and a friend. The motor fell off the boat and they took turns diving for it. The boat capsized and two drowned. One was able to cling to a tree that was in the water. He and the friend were rescued. I suspect they had been drinking.

My sister Louise married first and had a little girl named Yvonne. When she was just two years old, she drowned in the creek. That was a very sad time for all of us. After her husband Jay died, Louise confessed to me that for the rest of her life, Jay blamed her for Yvonne's death. Certainly, she didn't need his blame as I'm sure she heaped plenty of it on herself.

Once when I was about fifteen years old, my Hancock grandparents went out of town and asked me to water their yard and plants. I noticed a bat flopping around on the ground. It was around the time the rabid dog appeared in our back yard so I'm pretty certain the bat also had rabies. I used my grandfather's hoe and bludgeoned it to death.

I know this might sound strange, but I always felt like I had a great safety net and a support group. We had no father, yet the townspeople watched over us. Living in the small town of Taylor wasn't bad at all. We got involved in a lot of things going on at school and church. It was enjoyable to watch the town grow up a little later in my life, but when we were growing up, we mostly felt safe.

The saying that it takes a village to raise a child really applied to Taylor. I remember spending a lot of time with a teacher, Mrs. Perkins. I have a picture of myself and Janice with her in front of my Hancock grandparent's home. We were the talk of the town though because we weren't considered as religious as the community thought we should be. But with my mother working on Sundays, it was impossible for her to attend church. We attended the youth groups at the church like Mutual, but looking back on it, I'm glad we weren't expected to be so religious. I didn't want my whole life to be centered on religion.

My mother had strong morals and an outstanding set of values. Those things did not come from going to church. Her mother was very religious, self-righteous, and preached to us all the time. Yet she was not a nice person. On the other hand, my grandmother Kay never talked about religion. She lived it by being kind and loving. She was always a good teacher and a great example.

Life in Taylor wasn't always perfect. I recall an incident that happened that concerned everyone in town. One night Marilyn Hatch didn't return home from a church meeting. Her family went in search of her and found her on the side of the road. She had been the victim of a 'hit-and-run.' Marilyn was hurt quite badly and spent time in the hospital in McNary. People were certain it was one of the Lillywhite boys, but no one was able to prove it.

Perry Baldwin's oldest son got one of his legs caught in some type of machinery. It mangled his leg so badly that it had to be amputated at the knee. But this didn't have anything to do with a safety issue in the town. Accidents happen no matter where you live.

Uncle Quill and Grandma Kay felt compelled to discipline us when our mother wasn't around to witness some of our shenanigans. Grandma Kay was kind. She explained what we had done wrong and why we shouldn't do it again. Grandma Hancock disciplined us as well. But she was mean about dishing out punishment.

The Spudnut Shoppe in Show Low delivered their goods in Taylor and stopped by our house from time to time. Janice had a job at The Grill so she had spending money and once in a while, she bought half a dozen. She wouldn't let me or Corrine have even one doughnut to share. She ate every one of those doughnuts herself. I found it hard to forgive her because I wouldn't have considered doing that to her.

Janice and I did lots of things together. We were closer in age and quite honestly, I didn't want to run with the type of crowd with which Corrine chose to associate. However, it bothered me that Janice was not willing to share and that she lied about stealing Grandma Hancock's eggs.

Janice was small and delicate when she was younger. When she was in fourth grade, she was chosen to be a doll in the Christmas play. The only nice dress we had was mine. I was two years younger, but it fit so she got to wear it. It was a beautiful turquoise color with a grosgrain ribbon and it was the only nice dress I had ever owned. I behaved just like any child at that age. I threw a screaming fit.

Mr. Brain was my sixth-grade teacher and he lived alone in Shumway. One day I was with a group of people that included Jimmy White and Margie Reidhead. I don't know why, but Jimmy and Margie decided to break into Mr. Brain's home. After gaining entry, they trashed the house. It was the biggest mess I had ever seen. I was involved just because I was with the group. But I did not participate and in fact, it embarrassed me. I will never forget that and how it made me feel. I walked home by myself. Mr. Brain never discovered the culprits, but he left the area shortly after the incident.

Burt Hatch had some baby turkeys and for some reason a bunch of us decided to steal them. We took them to the house and fried and ate them. We made a huge mess and had to clean it up. Burt never found out who ran off with his turkeys.

I was a watermelon thief as well. If I remember right, we took those from the Shumways.

Chapter Three

Tribulations of a Teenager

When I was a teenager, Hatch Brother's Store was about the extent of the commerce in Taylor, Arizona. Also, there was a bar with small cabins surrounding it. Burt Hatch owned and rented the cabins. Like all small towns, we had a post office. It was in a small stone building just east of my Hancock grandparent's house and it served as the only gas station as well. Mrs. Larson was the post mistress. They also sold candy. She probably sold other things too, but I really didn't notice as I was only interested in the candy.

Later in my teen years, Leland Lillywhite and his family came to Taylor. They opened a competing grocery store that was dinky and had very little to offer.

I went to high school in Snowflake and I had to ride the bus. Our bus originated in Clay Springs and Janice and I decided we didn't like riding that bus even though we could catch it at the corner just west of our house. Instead, we walked to Center Street to catch a different bus.

It was always a treat to be able to get a ride to Snowflake to watch a movie at the theater. They only showed movies on Wednesdays and Saturdays.

I got a job working for Burt Hatch at The Grill Café. During the summer Burt picked me up at home and took me to work. When school was in session I walked to work from the high school. I was expected to stay until the restaurant closed, which was usually sometime between seven and eight PM. Then Burt enticed me to go over to the gym to watch a basketball game.

During the summer, Burt constantly had the radio on listening to ball games.

We never had that much to eat, so Louise, Janice and I were skinny girls. Corrine was a little chubby.

Doris, Louise, Afton, Corrine, and Janice Kay

Religion played a big part in my teen years. I bought into the dogma because that's all I heard and all I knew. All social activities centered on the LDS church. That's where all the parties and dances took place. There was no other church in town until much later. Of course, there was also the expectation from my mother that we would attend church and all of the church functions.

We stopped the job of cucumber-picking when we started high school; but I still wanted some spending money. Once in a while when family was in town from Mesa, I babysat. However, my primary job as a teenager was working at The Grill Café. I cooked, swept floors, did dishes and waited on tables. No one was hired to do just one thing. We learned to do everything. I made milkshakes and hamburgers. My mother had all the chili and stew made when I got there, but I had to cook hotdogs and make Coney Islands.

My teen years were spent swimming in the creek or the town pool, occasionally going to movies and generally just hanging out with my friends. Even in high school, the majority of my friends lived in Taylor. My best friend was Margie Reidhead.

I loved to read and I spent hours with my head in a book. At noon I liked to listen to a radio station called KKOB from Albuquerque, New Mexico. It played country western music.

When I was in high school, I was able to catch a ride to Pinetop with Grace Hatch. With the money I earned at The Grill, I purchased two nice dresses from Elaine's Dress Shop. One was black velvet and another was a beautiful rust color. I wore those dresses to the dances. I didn't have dates, but I danced all night with different boys.

I experienced my first kiss with Terrance "Shorty" Reidhead but it didn't take long for me to tire of him. He was all hands. One night on a date, he decided he could take liberties with me that I wasn't willing to give. When I told him to leave me alone and take me home, he informed me that if I wanted to go home, I could walk. I jumped out of his car and walked the two miles to my house. On my eighteenth birthday, he appeared at the Grill Café with a box of cherry chocolates, but I wasn't about to go out with him again.

I also dated a guy named Arvil Hunt who was four years older than me. He lived and worked in the logging industry in McNary and Maverick. He had a two-door Plymouth and he decided to teach me how to drive. We drove around and finally ended up on Pinedale Road. I had been driving, but now we were parked. Suddenly, my mother appeared out of nowhere wearing only her nightgown. She jerked the car door open and demanded that I get my butt home right now.

I dated a man named Robert Fulton for a time. He was also older than me. I was going to attend my senior prom with him. I had a beautiful short, pinkish caramel colored dress. However, I was unable to attend the prom because I was zapped with the measles.

Shortly thereafter, Arvil joined the service. I wrote to him and sent him pictures of me. He sent me lots of things from Korea, including some of my pictures painted on pieces of silk fabric.

For a short time after Arvil left, I dated a man who lived in Overgaard. He drove a truck for the loggers. His name was Tony Ashcroft. He was originally from New Mexico and he was a very nice guy. Tony was also four years older than me. I guess I was just drawn to the older men. My mother liked Tony and thought he was wonderful, but she wasn't thrilled about our relationship. I was dating him at Christmas and I remember he brought us a Christmas tree from Heber. He gave me a Christmas gift and got on my mother's good side by bringing her a gift as well. I had an interesting effect on the men I dated because Tony joined the service too. In my defense, the country was involved in the Korean Conflict at the time.

While Arvil and Tony were in the service, I met Jim McCarty. He swept me off my feet and when the others returned from the service, I was already married to Jim. Looking back on it now, I have some regrets about not waiting for Tony.

Tony smoked, but never offered a cigarette to me. He did offer me alcohol and I partook. When I was dating Jim McCarty, he took me to the Corral bar in Holbrook and the Navajo Inn in Show Low and, even though I was underage, I was served alcohol. My mother was dating a guy who worked with Jim and she and her date were with us one night at the Navajo Inn. Joe Baird ran the Navajo Inn. He sidled over to me and whispered softly in my ear "Don't you dare take another drink of that." It was quite embarrassing.

The year I graduated from high school the local Cucumber Festival was in its fifth year. This was a Labor Day event and included a parade and a night rodeo. Howard Ramsey and Burt Hatch decided I should run for Cucumber Queen. This was not a talent show, but a sales contest. I had lots of help selling chances for whatever the prize was, so I was the clear-cut winner. I was dating Jim McCarty by then. Jim and his friends bought lots of tickets, but on the weekend of the festival, he and his friend George Dalton, left for Nogales to watch the bull fights. The Arnold Pickle Company awarded me a nice western outfit and an Elgin watch. I rode on Howard Ramsey's beautiful horse in both the parade and the beginning of the rodeo. From that point forward, Jim referred to me as the Pickle Queen.

Doris Jean Kay as Pickle Queen

The school dress code required that we wear dresses, except on Fridays. We wore our dresses at mid-calf, but outside of school and on Fridays, we wore bell bottom pants or Levi's, which were both popular wardrobe items. We all had to have Levi's. All the girls loved them. It was very fashionable to roll them up and wear them with saddle shoes. I went through so many pairs of shoes. I didn't outgrow them; I wore them out.

We didn't have much money to buy clothes, so we were always grateful for the boxes of clothes sent from our aunt from Philadelphia. However, we were at her mercy for the style.

Hairstyles at the time were long and curly. All the girls had perms, including me, and I still perm my hair. It's straight as a board and hard to manage without one. I didn't like my hair. It never looked good and I just didn't like it. The thing I did like about my appearance was that I was skinny.

When I was a teenager, I had problems with my skin. Lots of pimples. Fortunately, around this time Bernice Larson opened a Merle Norman shop in her house. Margie and I rode the bus to her house and she taught us how to use the products. It was so nice to go there and get facials. My mother was willing to buy the Miracol and my face cleared up. I have used Merle Norman products ever since.

Western music was popular in Taylor. I loved "Blue Christmas", recorded by Ernest Tubb. When I was dating Tony Ashcroft, we went to Holbrook to see Slim Whitman. He was playing at the VFW hall. It was such a treat to hear him yodel.

When I was a teenager, the Jitterbug was the dance we adored. We waltzed, but we all loved to jitterbug.

I don't recall any great movies from my teenage years. I do remember seeing *Gone with the Wind,* in Snowflake, before I was a teenager. That movie was the talk of the town because there was cussing in the film, so of course I had to see it. When I was dating Joe Blair, we went to see it in Scottsdale. I was so glad to see it again after all those years.

I was close to my mother and our relationship was wonderful. I could talk with her about anything. However, she was strict with the discipline because she had four daughters to raise, and the way to make her unhappy was to shirk our chores. Our punishment was to complete them no matter what time of the day it was. I remember finishing chores late into the night if she came home to find we had not completed them.

I did try to be a good kid, but I'm not sure why. Looking back on it, I guess I didn't want to disappoint my mother. She was all I had and I couldn't bear to make her unhappy.

My relationships with Janice and Louise were harmonious, but Corrine was quite a different story. I don't recall that she was mean to Janice, but she picked on me constantly. One day, the last straw broke the camel's back and I beat the crap out of her. Our bed was in the living room. I wedged her between the mattress and the wall and beat the tarnation out of her. It seems she saw the light and never bothered me again. I guess she finally realized that I wasn't going to take it anymore.

Janice and I got along well. We were close in age and did lots of things together. She worked at the Grill Café before I did, but by the time I started, she was married.

Janice's husband, AJ Freeman, sold me my first car. It was an old stick shift and I believe it was a Chevy. I drove it to work in Show Low. I worked for Bill Cunningham. He had an office in the building that housed the theater. He did income tax. I don't think I ever made a payment on it, because I married Jim shortly after I 'bought' the car.

I wrote stories when I was a teenager and I was quite proud of that. Recently, Margie gave me something I wrote back then. I was never published and I did not get good grades. My mom wasn't that supportive because she was always working. When she was home, she had to cook and clean and do all those things you do to survive. She was exhausted all the time and rightly so.

I was painfully shy and bashful when I was a teenager as we never went anywhere so I wasn't exposed to people other than my family. Typically, I confided in my mother because I felt like I could tell her anything. I admired my Granddad Hancock greatly. He was the male figure in my life and he influenced me more than any other man I knew. He was such a good man. He stood up for what he believed in and I admired him a lot. I feel like he favored me and the time I spent with him I really enjoyed. When my children were small, I still spent a lot of time with him.

Burt Hatch was a huge influence on me. He let us work for him and we were always around his family. He gave us jobs and I thought that was marvelous of him to hire us to work for him, although we were hard workers. He took me to basketball and baseball games. I thought of him as a father figure. However, in later years, I came to think of Jim's father as a father figure. I loved that man.

James A. "Mac" McCarty

I did suffer some embarrassments. However, the most embarrassing thing that happened to me as a teenager was when my mother marched up the road and jerked me out of the car when I was with Arvil Hunt. Boy, was she a sight in her nightgown pulling me out of Arvil's car!

As I recall, I had a few nicknames. One of my friends called me 'Dodo.' It was Irene Bates and I never really cared for her because of that. Some people called me 'Dori' and a few of the boys called me 'Dorass.'

That was when I was in school. The worst nicknames I suffered through were after I married Jim. He called me Nasty Agnes and Lazy Doris, even going so far as to name boats using those nicknames. But his mother gave me the ultimate slam by making birthday and Christmas cards out with 'Dorass' on them. Perhaps she didn't like me because I married her precious boy.

Franklin Roosevelt was the president when I was a teenager. We had this radio my mother put on the table and we all had to come in and listen to his speeches about the war. My mother hung on every word he said and we took our roles as citizens supporting the war effort very seriously.

The Second World War was the most historic event that took place during my generation. All the men from the community were leaving to fight the war. It was frightening, especially since a lot of them never came home. We wondered if the war would come to United States soil. That's why my mother made us listen to the speeches and contribute all we could to the war effort. Our neighbors were leaving to fight and we needed to contribute. We collected aluminum foil off gum wrappers to save for scrap metal. The three Standifird boys left; two never returned. It was terrifying.

The happiest memory I have of my teen years is that I was alive and I loved it when I was able to do a few things. I thought I lost out on lots of things that others got to do because we had very little money. Although, now that I think about it, there wasn't really that much to do. The community was small and there weren't many activities available for teenagers.

We learned to roller skate and even to ice skate on a small pond. I had lots of fun with the kids who lived in Taylor swimming in the creek, attending church meetings and activities. We were all close back then.

My elementary school was small with a big hall in the middle. The hall was multi-functional with music and band classes held there, as well as basketball practice. In addition to the big hall, there were probably four classrooms. Each classroom held two grades. The school also had a big playground with swings.

The only time I received vaccinations is when they did it at school. That's the only time I saw a dentist as well. My sisters and I were not thrilled about this so we hid in the plum and gooseberry bushes hoping not to be found. Of course, my mother always knew where to find us so we were scooted off to school anyway.

One day I was told that I was going to have my picture taken at school. This was a frightening thing to me, as I couldn't fathom how it could take place. In my imagination it had to be something like getting a vaccine. My mother dressed me in a nice white dress and took extra time that morning to make sure I had nice ringlets in my hair. All the extra fuss didn't make me any happier about the photo shoot and I wasn't about to produce a smile.

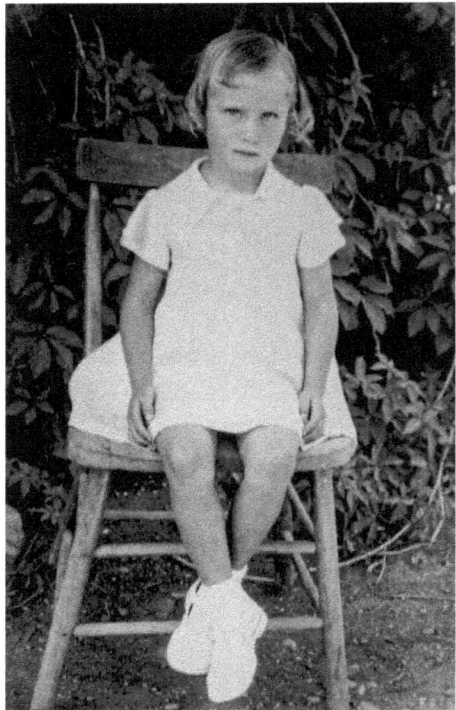

Doris Jean Kay c. 1940

Looking back at the photo now, it is quite funny. I'm sitting in a chair with a look of terror on my face.

The school had a kitchen that furnished lunches that could be purchased. My mother always made sure we had money for lunches because we couldn't go home for lunch as she wasn't there most of the time.

We didn't always have to walk to get where we were going. Perhaps we shouldn't have been so quick to hitch a ride. Grandma Kay's husband, the one we referred to as Uncle Joe, was a terrible driver. Once Uncle Joe stopped and asked if we wanted a ride. Not thinking about his lack of driving skills, we gladly jumped into the back of his truck and off he went. He let up on the clutch so hard that Corrine and Louise fell out of the truck. We were all the way to the school before he realized he had lost two of his passengers.

I was quite athletic, if I say so myself, and I participated in the track meets. I lived to play sports since I could beat all the boys. I liked the broad jump and the relay races because I could run and jump like a deer. I also played a lot of volleyball. In eighth grade I was a cheerleader, but I didn't try out in high school. I knew I didn't have much of a chance. The good Mormon girls from Snowflake always got to be the cheerleaders and I was not a good Mormon girl from Snowflake.

I liked music and really wanted to be in the band. We couldn't afford an instrument so I played the school-owned tambourine. Not that there was much of a part for a tambourine, but I always had fun when I got to play.

Out of necessity, my mother made most of our clothes including our underwear, which caused me one of the most embarrassing incidents of my young life. When Pearl Harbor was attacked in 1941, President Franklin Roosevelt called it a day that would live in infamy. Little did he know that shortly before that day, another day passed that would live in infamy. And just between the two of us, I'll forget Pearl Harbor long before I will ever forget that day.

Like others living in the long shadow of poverty, we didn't know how tough we had it. Others in our community were suffering financially and that tended to put our hardships in perspective. Everyone was scrambling to survive in the late 1930s. It was just that most of the other kids had a father to bring home the bacon and a mother to cook it.

I was the youngest daughter. By the time the hand-me-downs got to me, they were usually faded and worn to a frazzle. I hid my feelings of self-consciousness as best I could. I dreamed of having beautiful new clothes, but I knew Mom was doing everything she possibly could to help us get through the hard times. The closest I came to my dream of new clothes was when Mom made them herself. She made everything, right down to our slips and panties. She was a good seamstress, but quality materials were in short supply in the depression years. Several years in a row we did get a huge box of clothes from my Uncle Jess Kay's wife, Myrna. She sent them all the way from Philadelphia.

By the time I was in the third grade, I was like any other girl my age and I was becoming socially aware. Friendships were important, the strength of which rose and fell like mercury in the barometer with every social slight and event, real or imagined. We had a little band at school and I played the tambourine. We practiced after school.

A creek ran through the center of town and it made getting to and from school a challenge. There was a steel bridge, but it made the walk longer. When the creek was low, we could work our way across jumping from stone to stone. But in the spring time, the creek ran high because of the snows melting higher in the mountains around us. The most direct route was across the swinging bridge. You could see between the wooden slats and imagine falling through them into the icy waters below. It was old and scary.

The creek was running high one spring morning and so were my spirits. It was a bright and shiny day as I headed off to school in my newly crafted clothes. My mother had made them all and I felt great. The school day passed and I had fun playing the tambourine with my friends in the band. When it was time to leave, I joined my classmates, stood up, put my books under one arm and with my tambourine in my other hand, I headed out the door.

There were blue skies up above and the mood was a happy one. Spring flowers colored the fields. We chatted as we left the school. Then it happened. I felt a snap and instantly realized the elastic in my new under panties had broken. My panties were falling, but with my hands full of books and a tambourine, I was helpless to stop them. In an instant, feelings of joy turned to horror. In lurid slow motion, my panties dropped to the ground. I never anticipated such a disaster and I was frozen with fear. They hit the ground as my ruby red face radiated my terror. I did the only thing I could think of and walked out of them. And I just kept on walking and I never looked back.

My walk quickly turned into a run. I didn't dare take the swinging bridge. I ran all the way to the steel bridge and reached it long before the other kids. When I finally got home, I was panting and panty-less. I relived the tragedy over and over that night like a recurring nightmare. With each replay, I suffered overwhelming embarrassment.

The following morning, I begged my mother to let me stay home from school. There was no way I could face my friends – if they were indeed still my friends. My mother made me go. The day in school passed without a single word from a single person. There was some relief in that. And since that day, no one has said a word to me about the incident. To this day, more than seventy years later, no one has mentioned the events of that afternoon. I don't know where the panties went. I still think I'd die if someone came up to me, hand extended, panties tightly in its grasp, and said, "Excuse me, but I believe you left these at school one day."

Chapter Four

School Daze

Being the youngest meant I was usually home alone after school, which made me a latchkey kid, although we didn't lock the door. The first thing I did when I got home was to scrounge around for something to eat. After all, I was a growing girl and I was starving. The cupboard was usually bare, making it a long, agonizing wait for my mother to get home from work to prepare dinner.

During my school years I had some memorable teachers. Being a small school, the teachers did double duty. Mary Shumway was my first and second grade teacher and I liked her. She was a so-called old maid, meaning she wasn't married at an age everyone thought she should be, and she was strict with us. She taught me to read and write. I also really liked my third and fourth grade teacher, Idell Solomon. But I just loved my eighth-grade teacher, Brown Capps. He was by far my favorite teacher, although he always smelled like cigarette smoke, which I could hardly stand. Nonetheless, I was able to ignore the smell because he was a good teacher and he was lots of fun. He played the clarinet in class and for our school dances. He was the nicest, funniest and smelliest man.

I was not a great student, but I still liked school. My favorite subjects were math, history and especially spelling. To me, learning the new words and printing them out was sublime. Yet I excelled at reading. I loved taking turns reading aloud from the chosen book. In fact, one year I received an award for reading the most books. One book of which I was particularly fond was about the Twin Cities, Minneapolis/St. Paul, in Minnesota. Although I can't remember the name of the book, I loved it so much that I would give anything to read that book again. Poetry was also something I enjoyed, with "The Village Blacksmith" by Henry Wadsworth Longfellow one of my favorites.

Although I didn't mind school at all, I was always glad when they dismissed us for the summer. We had lots of things we could do in summer that didn't keep us tethered to a classroom.

My mother wanted us to go to school, but she was never home to help me with homework. Sometimes it seemed like she really didn't care if I went to school or even graduated. By the time I began my education, she was working so hard and was always so tired that she didn't have the energy to take much interest in what I was doing in school. Although the other girls took piano lessons, I didn't get to do that because times were tough and someone had to pay the piano teacher.

World War II was at full throttle during my grade school days. When anything significant happened, the administration called us into assembly for the announcement. It was a frightening time for me. I thought each time there was an announcement that they would tell us we were being invaded by our Japanese enemies; and I didn't like rice.

The high school I attended was in Snowflake with the student body consisting of kids from Snowflake, Taylor, Show Low, Heber, Overgaard, Pinedale and Clay Springs. Although I dated a few guys from Show Low, including Scott Finney and Jimmie Stock, they could be characterized as wild and were more than I wanted to take on. I learned to stay away from them.

The LDS church offered religious education seminary classes at the high school. My mother thought I should attend and all my friends were there so I took seminary for all four years of high school.

Physical education was a requirement when I was in high school and I liked my P.E. teacher, Mrs. Bates. She was a lot of fun and I enjoyed P.E. My high school had a girls baseball team, which was affiliated with the P.E. class and it competed against other schools. I was a fielder and managed to catch a few fly balls in my day.

The Snowflake kids treated everyone else terribly. They didn't want anything to do with the rest of us and thought they were much better than we were. They certainly didn't like the Show Low people, with the exception of Jackie Wolford and Karly Smith. Those girls tried out for cheerleader and were very popular. If you weren't a cheerleader, you didn't have much to recommend you.

During my days in high school, we had a fall Harvest Ball, which was the equivalent of Homecoming at other schools. Each class nominated someone to be Harvest Ball Queen and my freshman class nominated me. They did everything they could short of stuffing the ballot box to get me elected. My cousin, Bill Baldwin, was two years older than me, but supported me and brought in a fair number of votes. Usually, the senior class nominee was elected, but not that year. I won and it set in motion my experience as an outcast at school. Most of the girls avoided me like the plague after that, which I can only surmise was due to my ability to harvest votes.

My senior year I was class secretary and I enjoyed that tremendously. Bill Bryant was president and Jackie Wolford was vice-president. After high school, it was my job to help organize the reunions and find the kids that were in my class, which I also found gratifying.

I didn't like school, but I loved certain subjects like history and geography. It was interesting and thought-provoking to learn about places I had never been and historical happenings that shaped the world. However, I missed a lot of my classes because I was sickly when I was in high school. I had both my tonsils and appendix removed during that four-year period.

Math and shorthand were also subjects I enjoyed, but I was not the best of students. My mother didn't have time to monitor whether or not I got my homework done, so I didn't trouble myself to complete it and then hand it in. It bothered me that my grades weren't good, but somehow, I couldn't correlate that fact with my approach to homework.

Mr. Levine, who was the oddball history instructor, was my favorite teacher. He came from New York and I think he might have been Jewish, but ended up marrying a Snowflake girl and joining the LDS Church. He was quite funny. If you said a word in his class, he pelted you with a piece of chalk, which I found rather refreshing.

When I was fifteen or sixteen, I ditched school with Janice and Margie Reidhead. Janice blocked out that day entirely and still denies that she was with us, but she was. We decided we wanted to try to smoke but we didn't have any cigarettes. We must have been going for the "cool" factor because we substituted some weeds that had holes in them and lit them. That didn't work out well for us and I never tried to smoke again.

Show Low was in the Snowflake School District, therefore Show Low students attended high school in Snowflake. They were bussed to school every day. Although Lakeside, which was much closer than Snowflake, had a high school, it was not accredited. This led some kids from Lakeside and Pinetop to move in with relatives in Snowflake and Taylor so they could attend high school in Snowflake.

I graduated in May of 1952. It was a dressy affair and I remember I wore a gold two-piece suit with a white blouse. Graduation took place on a Friday and Baccalaureate was on the Sunday before. Baccalaureate was the ceremony acknowledging our completion of seminary. Seminary is a religious education program for youth of The Church of Jesus Christ of Latter-day Saints. In my day, you could participate in Baccalaureate if you completed three years of Seminary. The classes took place in a building adjacent to the high school, owned by the LDS church, and if you participated, you replaced a high school class with a seminary class.

My graduation class consisted of forty-two students. The administration wanted everyone to participate in the graduation ritual. Some sang in the choir, some played in the band. I was class secretary, so I had a speaking part and although I was nervous, I got through it. However, I don't remember a thing that I said. Aunt Stella's family even came over from Winslow. We celebrated at home afterward, with me receiving quite the haul of gifts from friends and family.

My mother was born in Taylor at her parent's home on January 19, 1911. She grew up in Taylor and spent a lot of time in the summer at Sheep's Crossing in the White Mountains. She and her siblings were expected to help their father with the sheep, but there was also time for fishing, swimming in the cold mountain streams, chasing squirrels and living a carefree life. My mother described herself as a tomboy, riding mules and climbing trees with the best of them.

Mom was quite a dancer and spent lots of time at a place in Show Low called the Blue Moon. I think she had a bit of a wild streak, which I'm sure endeared her to her mother. She was pregnant when she married at the age of 17, never completing high school. My dad was eight years her senior.

My dad drove a truck all of his working life, spending a lot of time in

Afton Kay c. 1926

Farmington, New Mexico. He began drinking heavily while in Farmington as it was easy to purchase bootlegged liquor. Later he worked in Hillside, a small mining town near Prescott, Arizona where he drove a truck for a mining company. I was told he died in Prescott as a result of hernia surgery. I saw his death certificate years later and realized that he died of "acute alcoholism, hepatic insufficiency and delirium tremens."

Twice, while my dad was working in Hillside, my mother took Janice and me to visit him there. Louise and Corrine had to stay behind with my mom's sister, Leah. We drove to Holbrook and took the train to Flagstaff. Someone met us there and drove us to Hillside. On one occasion the Santa Maria River was flooding and we had to wait on the other side of the river before we could cross and get into Hillside. Even though I was only four when my father died, I remember these trips and crying on the train because I was scared.

On the first visit, my parents went into the bedroom and never came out. The second night of that trip the adults left all of us kids at a boarding house and went dancing. But on the second trip, my dad left with his girlfriend and never came back. I remember my mother cried and cried. Her life with my father was sad and miserable.

My sisters and I saw my mother cry a lot over my father, but she never said anything about him or how she felt when he died. I do remember my mother crying many, many times after his death. The most painful thing I remember about my mother was when my dad died. Everything before and after could just not compare to that tragedy.

She kept everything bottled inside, and after realizing that, I feel really bad. The bad things I heard about my dad came from my Aunt Leah, my mother's sister, so I suspect my mother's side of the family did not like him. My Uncle Quill and his daughter, Fern, were relatives on my father's side so they never said anything derogatory to us about him. It was sad for me and my sisters when he died because my mother was so heartbroken. But thinking back on it, I wonder if her heartbreak had more to do with his treatment of her.

When my father died, my mother was forced to find work, although she was able to stay at home until I started first grade. At that time, she went to work in Snowflake at The Grill Café which was owned at that time by my Uncle Wren Kay. She was always very busy and hard at work while I was growing up.

She contracted the flu once and we thought she was going to die. She lay in bed for days so sick she couldn't get up. No one was able to help so my sisters and I took care of her.

My happiest memories of my mother were my memories from Christmas. We had so much fun around Christmas. I remember that more than anything. But even on Saturdays when we had to work so hard to get everything done, we had lots of fun. My mother knew how to make things fun. Grandma Kay was always around and she certainly knew how to have a good time as well.

My mother was a nice-looking, single woman who had a lot of friends. In fact, people came to The Grill and talked with her and teased her. One evening, Frank Gardner stopped by the house and asked her to go for a drive. Off they headed on the back road to Shumway. Frank ran off the road and almost wrecked the car. Of course, people teased Mom unmercifully about Frank trying to make out with her and losing control of the car. Uncle Speed and Imogene Maxwell called my mother Uncle Frank for years because of that incident.

The Grill Café was the happening place in town. It was open for breakfast, lunch and dinner and my mother did the majority of the cooking, in addition to making at least four pies each day. All the kids my age liked to eat lunch there. They would come in and go directly to the pie keeper to grab the piece they wanted before they placed their lunch order for fear that they wouldn't get the piece of pie they wanted. Invariably, The Grill ran out of pie before day's end. I never got pie because by the time I got to work there wasn't a slice in the place.

Mom grew up in the LDS Church, but she never preached about it to us. We said a prayer at night and we said a blessing on our food before we ate. She made sure we went to church but she never discussed religion. She was not a religious fanatic. In her later years, Louise and Janice pressured her into going to the temple to be sealed to my father. She didn't want to do that, but they were pushy and forceful daughters where the church was concerned. Her reluctance was palpable. She believed that she would be married to him for eternity and he had treated her so poorly that she couldn't bear the thought of it.

My mother died January 20, 1991, the day after her eightieth birthday. She had a stroke and my sisters and I were unable to care for her, so she was in a nursing home in Show Low. She hated it there and asked daily to go home, which broke my heart. I think she must have had another stroke, because for the last week of her life, she didn't know we were there with her. She is buried in Taylor next to my father. I'm not sure that's where she wanted to be, but we didn't know where else to put her.

After Mom had a stroke and before she went to the nursing home, I went to Taylor once a week to clean her house. We had such a great time laughing and talking. One week we called my sister Corrine and the next week Corrine called us. I made whatever my mother wanted for lunch that day. Sometimes she wanted something special. I had such a great time and I found out all kinds of things I didn't know. She even talked about my dad some. I liked the fact that she expressed her opinion about people and things after she had her stroke. She didn't do that very often before the stroke and I assume the stroke caused her to lose some of her inhibitions.

My mother taught me how to take care of myself and how to work hard. She wanted us to look nice and clean at all times. My hair was always in ringlets or braids. It was just very important to her that we pass muster with the community, as she was a single mother raising four girls and raising them under a microscope. But I remember her laughing all the time. Even through the sad times she laughed and I loved that about her.

My father was born in Taylor, I assume in my Grandmother Kay's house. He was never home when I was little and died when I was four, so I don't know a great deal about him. He grew up in Taylor. From the pictures I've seen of him, he was a handsome man, five feet ten or eleven and fairly muscular with dark curly hair. He liked women and women liked him. In fact, he had the audacity to bring home candy his girlfriend had made. He actually told us she had made it.

In spite of his faults, everyone seemed to love my dad. He was described to me by relatives and friends as a fun-loving guy who laughed all the time and loved to tell a joke. In other words, he was a good old party guy. He always had a steady job, but rarely sent any money home to my mother. Perhaps he spent it on wild women or the candy maker.

John Henry Kay

My father drank to excess. The few times he was at home when I was small, he was drunk. I did not inherit that particular trait because I was never into the drinking thing. I married a man who liked to drink as well, another reason I don't really like to drink. My most painful memory of my dad was that he made my mother cry. And she cried a lot.

My father wasn't home much, although I have a vivid memory of one visit. On his way home from Hillside to Taylor around Christmas one year, he saw a gunny sack in the road and stopped to pick it up. It was full of Brazil nuts and we ate them all. However, when he was home, he just partied all the more. He really wasn't much of a father and because he was never home, I didn't really know him. He wasn't religious even though as a young man I'm sure my Grandmother Kay made him attend church. After he grew up, I don't think he ever went to church. He was an alcoholic and so self-involved that he couldn't be a good father or husband. I did not want to be like my dad. He had feelings only for himself. I did not want to be that kind of person, and unfortunately, I don't remember anything good about him.

I was told he had hernia surgery in 1938 in Prescott, Arizona and died in the hospital there. I recently saw a copy of his death certificate and it states he died of "acute alcoholism, hepatic insufficiency and delirium tremens." I guess no one wants to tell small children their dad was a hopeless drunk. He was 35 years old when he died. My mother was 28 and was left with four children. He was buried in the Taylor cemetery. At that time, it was the most desolate looking cemetery, located on an old dried-up piece of land. When Reed Hatch became bishop of the LDS ward in Taylor, which he was for a number of years, he did a lot for Taylor, including taking the Boy Scouts to the White Mountains to dig up a bunch of spruce trees. They planted them in the Taylor cemetery after I got married.

Just before Reed Hatch died, Janice and I went to visit him. He told us we should not judge our father for never being at home. He told us there was no work in Taylor and that he had to leave in order to find work. That might have been true, but he never sent my mother any money. He used it to drink and party with other women while he had four children and a wife at home.

I don't know how my parents met. Taylor was a small town and I'm sure everyone hung around together. I think he might have dated my mother's sister, Emily, first. Emily was closer to his age. My mother was seven months pregnant when they finally married. I know nothing about their courtship. They got married in Gallup, New Mexico. In Arizona there was a waiting period between getting a license and getting married. That was not true in New Mexico, so lots of Arizona people married in New Mexico.

I'm concerned about alcoholism being passed to my prodigy through the Kay side of my family. Strokes are prevalent on the Hancock side and arthritis comes from the Kay side. My grandmother Kay had arthritis. Grandma Hancock had diabetes and my mother ended up with it after her stroke. Just before my sister Louise died, she found out she had diabetes as well.

James D. (Jim) McCarty came to the White Mountains in 1952 with Isbell Construction Company to build Show Low Lake Dam. He and the crew spent a lot of time in The Grill Café, which was where I worked. I was a senior in high school when I began dating Jim. My friend, Margie Reidhead, was dating Jim's friend and co-worker, George Dalton.

Jim lived in Show Low at The Boarding House. It was owned by Joe & Midge Kay and had a common kitchen for the boarders to share. Margie and I fancied ourselves great cooks and one day Jim and George asked us to make them an enchilada dinner. Off we went to the store to buy our ingredients. We came back and made a huge mess. After dinner, the guys insisted we go to a movie. We insisted we should clean up the mess in the kitchen. Jim and George were quite persuasive and promised they would clean the kitchen later. By the time they had taken us home to Taylor and returned to Show Low, it was too late. Midge Kay gave me grief for years because I left that kitchen such a mess. I apologized and explained what happened, but it made no difference to her.

Chapter Five

Matrimony

I graduated high school in May of 1952. I continued working at The Grill Café until I married Jim on April 18, 1953. We rented a small cabin in Show Low and set up housekeeping. The cabin was one of two and was situated on five acres on the highway between Show Low and Lakeside. The property was owned by the Wilburns.

We were there for only two months when we moved to Ash Fork, in northern Arizona. I considered our first home to be in Ash Fork. There were hardly any rentals and we found this tiny, little house to rent. It was filthy and I worked my fingers to the bone to clean it up. A week later we found a nice duplex in the center of town. It was a one-bedroom with a living room, kitchen and bath. We lived in the duplex until we moved to Phoenix in September.

By the time we moved to Phoenix, Jim's sister June and her husband, Walter, had purchased the Rainbow Bread route in the White Mountains and they moved to Show Low. We rented their home in Phoenix. It was near Bethany Home Road in a very nice neighborhood with nice homes. We weren't able to stay there for long because the house sold. We rented another small home and that's where we were living when our oldest daughter, Liz, was born.

Jim and I moved around like nomads because he had to follow construction work. It wasn't an easy thing in those days, moving all the time. Our belongings were put on the back of one of Isbell's trucks and moved to the next job. I was nervous about having enough money to take care of a child. Construction paid better than some jobs, but it certainly wasn't steady. On top of that, Jim wasn't very motivated. I had to make sure he got out of bed in time to get to work and that wasn't easy. If he was late, he blamed me and he was mad.

He was not present when Liz was born. He had not been working for a while and finally had a job. His father told me Jim was not going to take off work just to be with me while I was in labor. However, his parents, Jim and Mildred, were with me so I was not alone.

It was difficult to get used to being married and traveling all over Arizona. I made my life around Jim's construction buddies and their wives. Those were the people we knew and with whom we socialized. My friends were Emo Kirkland, Gladys Holden, Jane Dalton, Eddie Witt, Midge Kay and her daughter Susie.

When we lived in Ash Fork, there was absolutely nothing to do. It was a railroad town with one tiny grocery store, a few bars and a few motels. There were more stores in Williams, which was about 20 miles away, so Emo and I took turns driving to Williams. We'd spend the day grocery shopping and having lunch. The guys went to work early, so I'd go over to Emo's house. We were both pregnant and we'd get in her bed because we were cold.

Doris Kay McCarty

At the time, Midge and Joe Kay lived in Seligman. There was a nice little restaurant there, and about once a week, Jim and I drove there to eat dinner. We went to Prescott for the Fourth of July rodeo. It was a big deal and there were many things to do on Whiskey Row. We also spent time at Granite Dells, which is a beautiful place, covered with water and granite boulders near Prescott. You could swim there, but by then I was a big, fat pregnant thing, so I missed the opportunity.

It was hard to be away from my family that first year. I missed them and they missed me. We were a close family, because what did you have in a small community like Taylor, Arizona but family? I kept in touch as I could and Jim and I visited Taylor a couple of times when we were living in Ash Fork. I found myself pregnant shortly after I got married and I was craving all kinds of food. On one of our visits to Taylor, Granddad Hancock gave me half a gunny sack full of carrots. My mother was living alone and we stayed with her.

Back to Show Low we moved in May of 1954. We rented one of the Reidhead's duplexes, which was next to their sawmill. Later, we moved to a small home LeRoy Ellsworth owned, adjacent to his apple orchard. But we really liked the property we lived in when we first married and an opportunity presented itself about this time. Mr. Wilburn worked for Arizona Public Service and the Wilburns wanted to move back to Phoenix. We were able to purchase the property and made payments to the Wilburns.

We moved into one of the cabins and began adding on to make it into a house. The cabin was basically one room with a bathroom. We enlarged it so that there was a living room with a fireplace and a separate kitchen and bedroom. We decided to add a second story with two bedrooms.

Jim and I did most of the work for the addition. Joe Kay built the cabinets for the kitchen and helped out a little from time to time. Our first child, Liz, was about fourteen months old by then and I was pregnant with our second child. After we got the stairs built, Liz decided they were hers. She hopped up and down the stairs all day long. One day she tumbled down the stairs and landed in a box full of pieces of lumber. She wasn't hurt but it scared us all.

We had lots of fun building our first home. We even hung all the drywall while I was pregnant. I never thought it looked right and assumed we had done it wrong. I guess when you do the work, you can see every flaw. It was a nice home and we had enough room for both girls. When our third daughter was born four years later, there was still plenty of room.

David Foil and Jerry Hall developed a subdivision just north of Show Low in Navajo County. It was called Show Low Country Club. Jim did a lot of work for them and ended up with a couple of lots in return. We decided to build a new home there and moved into it in November of 1964. It was a large home (5,000 square feet) which included a large basement with a bomb shelter. Those were the days when people thought that would save them. The house was on the golf course and had a large kitchen with plenty of room to cook and bake.

Liz, Kathy, Victoria, Jim, and Doris McCarty

Jim's father had a big influence on both of us. Jim was an ambitious man, but his father was constantly pushing him to do more, be more. Jim wanted to own his own business and his dad was right there with support. His dad was so much fun.

Jim didn't want to work construction for the rest of his life. One day he came home early from a job. He had been fired for turning a Caterpillar over. He was determined, from then on, that he was going to own his own business. Show Low and the surrounding area was just starting to grow. People were buying vacation homes, so he decided to start making and manually installing septic tanks. His dad borrowed ten thousand dollars for him so he could get started in his business.

He was a hard worker. He couldn't afford new equipment, so most of what he had was crappy. Nothing ever started, so I had to pilot while he pulled the equipment to get it started.

Jim was always trying to earn extra money in order to get ahead. At one point, after working all day on his own projects, he jumped in a truck and drove to Globe with a load of dry cleaning. He brought the clean clothes back with him. Ken and Dorothy Heppard owned the dry-cleaning company. They had two children, a boy and a girl.

Although I did a lot of work to help Jim in his efforts, I considered myself a stay-at-home mom. I went to work as a dental assistant for Gordon Langston when Jim and I decided to divorce. I had to take a class to become certified to take dental x-rays.

Later I moved to Phoenix and went to work for American Greetings stocking cards in a Smitty's grocery store near my house. It involved setting up displays and making sure all the cards were put up and cared for. I worked three to four days per week for five to six hours per day. It was a large card department and I had lots of fun working there. I met lots of nice people who worked there and still stay in contact with some of them. Eva Durrell was a war bride who came over from Germany with her husband. She worked in cosmetics.

In high school I was working for Burt Hatch at the Grill Café in Snowflake. I walked from school at 2:00 and stayed until Burt took me home after we closed at 8:00. I cooked hamburgers, cheeseburgers and chili dogs and waited on tables. Burt had a fountain, so I made milk shakes and sodas. My mother made the chili, and lots of other things that I just had to warm up before serving. She made a mean stew every day and taught me to make oyster stew. I wasn't old enough to sell alcohol, so someone else had to do that. We only served beer. Jim always ordered beer when he came in and I couldn't serve him.

At one point Burt hired a woman who decided she was going to make her mark by changing lots of things. It really caused an uproar. She started slicing tomatoes and getting things ready ahead of time. Then we just sat around waiting for a crowd that never appeared. I tried to tell her it wasn't going to work, but I was just a kid and she wasn't going to listen to me. Burt finally had to take control again and get her to stop acting like the precursor to McDonald's.

Jim started calling me every night when he didn't come into The Grill. We talked for a long time and then he started asking me out to movies. He was fun and funny. But he always had a bottle of whiskey with him.

Jim was born in Vernal, Utah on February 16, 1931. He spent time in Indiana with his paternal grandparents as well as time in Chicago. Eventually, his parents moved to Phoenix to try to get his mother's asthma under control. He graduated from North Phoenix High School along with lots of friends with whom he kept in contact for years. His interests were diverse, and he enjoyed doing and seeing anything within his means. We went to Nogales to bull

Virginia and John Linde

fights with George Dalton. We watched lots of movies.

Jim kept in touch with a few of his high school friends for his entire life. One was John Linde. We were living in Phoenix when our oldest daughter was born, and I spent lots of time with John's wife, Virginia. Gene Suiter was another good high school friend, but they didn't stay in touch as much.

I think the thing that attracted me most about Jim at the time I met him is that he wasn't from the area. I found him fascinating. Our first date was a movie. He always had something going on and I usually got into trouble for it.

Hangin' Tree Bar

We used to go dancing at the Navajo Inn and Bill's Bar. Once Jim bought a drink for me, and Joe Baird came over to the table and said "You little shit. You're not supposed to be drinking, so don't drink anymore." He scared me to death and I didn't drink again there. I was only eighteen years old. Years later, Jim and I ended up owning that bar. We changed the name to The Hangin' Tree.

Jim asked me to marry him and when I said yes, he asked my mother if he could marry me. I was sitting there and I'll never forget what she said. "I'm telling you that you had better be good to her if she marries you." He always liked my mother.

We knew each other about eight months before we got married. We drove to Gallup, New Mexico on a Saturday morning and went to the courthouse to get a marriage license. We got married there at the courthouse and it wasn't the most romantic place. He had been married previously, and at the time, Arizona had a law that you had to wait a year before you could marry again.

Attendees at the wedding were Jim's parents, Jim and Mildred McCarty, my mother, Afton Kay, my sister Louise Hatch, my sister Janice and her husband AJ Freeman. George Dalton, Jim's buddy from work, rounded out the wedding party. I wore an off-white dress with a pleated skirt and a hat. Jim wore a suit and tie. I was eighteen and Jim was twenty-one.

Afton Kay, Doris, Jim, Mildred, and "Mac" McCarty

We really didn't have a honeymoon. We rented a little cabin in Gallup and spent the night there. We went out to eat and I don't remember doing anything special. He had to be back to work on Monday morning.

Before we got married, some friends had a Chiverie party for us in Show Low. A Chiverie is a mock serenade with kettles, pans, horns, and other noisemakers given for a newly married couple. Their version was a wagon with tin cans tied behind it, and inside was a pot full of beer with hot dogs around the beer, so it looked like poop. They teased us, played music, and made us walk up and down the main street begging for money with a tin cup. My friends and family had a bridal shower for me in Taylor, but the Chiverie was a party to humiliate a soon-to-be-married couple.

I got along very well with my new father-in-law. He liked me and was really good to me. My mother-in-law liked me in the beginning, but it didn't take her long to decide that no one would be good enough for Jimmy, her only son. It didn't matter how hard you worked to be a good wife. She was hard to please.

Mildred McCarty

The most arguments we had were over money. We didn't have any and if it hadn't been for my mother, we might have starved. She gave us a lot of food and bought a lot of clothes for my girls. She was very helpful.

I was the one who always apologized when we fought. He never apologized. I don't know if he wasn't sorry or he just didn't have it in him to say he was sorry. Sometimes, later in our marriage, I stayed mad at him for days. Getting along with Jim was not always an easy task.

In Show Low, the minute you moved to a new ward of the LDS church, they sent home teachers and visiting teachers. Religion was not important in our marriage. Jim wasn't about to go to church. I went alone sometimes, but he did go to church when Liz and Victoria were blessed. When it came time to bless Kathy, he stayed at the lake and I went alone. That might have been his way of saying "Maybe you shouldn't do this."

One night, Almon Owens and Mitchell Bushman made an appointment to come to the house. They arrived with a blackboard and began a religious presentation. It lasted over two hours and both Jim and I were quite upset about it. They were never invited back.

One day I went to Nick's Market in Show Low to purchase groceries. I was driving a station wagon. An employee offered to carry my groceries to the car. I opened the back of the station wagon to reveal a pile of chicken feathers. Jim and I, along with A.J. & Janice Freeman, had stolen someone's chickens and taken them home in the station wagon. I had forgotten about it, and in this moment, I was caught in the act.

Jim and I traveled quite a bit. He loved Arizona and every chance he got, he packed us in the car and took off on a road trip. We saw a lot of Arizona that way and a few times, his parents accompanied us. We didn't take many vacations, but we did take Liz and Victoria to the San Diego Zoo. In the summer of 1968, we were in California when Robert Kennedy was assassinated. We went to Uvalde, Texas for the funeral of one of Jim's employees who was murdered on a job in Tucson.

Jim loved the water and we had some kind of boat most of our married life. It began with a Biesemeyer boat and each time we bought a new boat, the new boat was bigger. We had a small cabin cruiser he named Lazy Doris. The next was a little bigger cabin cruiser he named Nasty Agnes, a charming moniker for me. After Jim did some work for the Park Service at Lake Powell, he couldn't live without a 55 foot house boat he christened Scorpio, after my astrological sign. It was on Lake Mead for a time but later it was moved to Lake Powell and there it remained. The girls and I spent a lot of time on that boat in the summers.

At some point, Jim bought a small plane. We traveled around in that quite a bit. In the summers, he flew back and forth between Show Low and Page, Arizona to spend time with us on the boat. He also used it to fly to and from his jobsites around the state.

Chapter Six

Embracing Change

Jim and I divorced in 1977 after 24 years of marriage. For a time, we might as well have been married because we still spent lots of time together. In the divorce settlement, I got the house in the country club, a car and $250,000. Jim kept the $250,000 and used it to fund the various developments he did in Show Low. I cannot complain because I received nice monthly checks for the interest and I still receive them to this day, 40 years later. I promptly sold the house in the country club and purchased a doublewide mobile home in Fairway Park. Kathy was 16 when we divorced and Jim was intent on mending fences. He gave her a car for Christmas.

I was unhinged by the divorce and went out on the town a lot with my friend, Stormi Langston. I know I worried Kathy, but I was just beside myself and unable to think straight. I had gone from my mother's house to living with Jim and I didn't know what to do next.

After Kathy graduated from high school in 1978, I purchased a new home in the Tatum and Shea area in Phoenix. I spent two years working for Smitty's grocery as a greeting card merchandiser and taking classes in floral arranging, in case I ever wanted to open my own flower shop.

Eventually, I met a man from Safford, Arizona. His name was Joe Blair. We traveled a lot. He was a commodities broker and he flew to Des Moines, Iowa quite a bit. I was invited to tag along. We took a trip by train to the Copper Canyon in Chihuahua, Mexico. We traveled around New Mexico. I really enjoyed a trip we made to Ruidoso.

I moved to Safford in 1980 when I invested in a large feedlot with Joe as my partner. He was nothing like Jim in the money department. Jim was quite frugal and Joe had a hard time living within his means. My daughter, Victoria, and her husband Vernon, moved to Safford to help with the feedlot. The best part of that was that I was able to spend time with my grandson, Alex. Although the enterprise was interesting, Joe was drinking the profits and killing the calves, so I moved on.

In 1982, I was back in Show Low. I began dating Larry Witt. He was a few years younger than me and had been my paperboy when Jim and I lived in Ash Fork. Witt had lived in Show Low for years and he and his wife, Mary, ran in the same circles as Jim and me. Witt's wife Mary had died in a car accident shortly after I moved back to Show Low. We married in May of 1984.

Larry "Witt" and Doris Witt

Witt was working for Salt River Project in St. Johns at the time.

Shortly after we married, Witt bought a logging truck and hauled logs for the next eight years. While Larry logged, we lived in Canby, a small town in northern California for a time. We arrived in late spring and left after Thanksgiving. We lived in a fifth wheel we purchased from Jim and we made some good friends, Buckey and Josie Bass. I helped Witt by taking care of all the bookwork and paying the bills. The spotted owl brought the logging phase to an end. After he sold his truck, he began hauling excavating and landscape material for local companies including Perkins Cinders. He retired from Perkins to take care of me when I started having health problems.

Witt is an extremely talented artist and has won numerous awards for his work in leather. He gave up that hobby for wood turning. His segmented and single-piece woodturnings have been displayed in art galleries across the country. I loved helping him by shining the finished product. I had to rush him to the hospital a few times when he cut off a finger or two. I also helped with his physical therapy by throwing things at him to improve the dexterity in his hands. Perhaps he'll move faster next time.

Witt

I love animals and have had many cats over the years. I preferred female cats. I had a few dogs when Jim and I were married. One turned out to be a coyote pup who finally figured out he didn't want to be domesticated and he ran away. Witt and I have had schnauzers. We started out with a female. Witt finally named her Damnit because that is what I kept saying when we first got her. I was not used to a puppy running around chewing on everything. And don't get me started on the potty training. When Damnit died, we were both heart-broken and acquired two dogs, Fritzy and Noodles. The next one was Sadie and now we have Katy.

Over the years, I have done a number of things to keep myself busy and out of trouble. I love working outside in the yard. Flowers and plants have been a part of my life for as long as I can remember. I always had a very colorful yard and my house is full of plants. I helped both Jim and Witt in their businesses, including driving a garbage truck and sewage pump truck. They were both delightfully pungent experiences. I kept the books for both of them as well.

I was very involved in the girls' school classes. I made treats for all the kids on special occasions, like Valentine's Day. I was an officer in the PTA and a homeroom mom. The PTA members always made special things for the teachers for holidays and birthdays.

In 1976, I began working as a dental assistant and took classes for x-ray certification in that field. However, I found that staring into gaping mouths and holding down reluctant patients was not my calling.

As far as accomplishments in my middle years, I would say it was getting through so many surgeries. I remember the first one I had in Flagstaff. They put me under for the hysterectomy and it was so frightening to realize I was going under. I felt so great when I came out of the surgery and everything was okay. When I went back to Flagstaff for my post-op check-up, all three of my daughters went along. On the trip there, Liz mentioned that I had gotten really crabby since the surgery. Apparently, she was too young to understand what going through menopause meant and that a hysterectomy brings it on all at once.

I have had a good life, with mostly happy times. However, I have overcome some difficult emotional periods as well – my divorce, the deaths of my mother, brothers-in-laws, and sisters and several surgical procedures. Yet, I'm in relatively good health.

I have never shared this with anyone until now. I never told Jim, but my daughters need to know what happened to me. When Jim started his business, he bought pipe from a company in Globe, Arizona. The company sent a representative to Show Low to take orders. One night when Jim was out of town, the representative showed up at our home. This was not unusual. However, when I opened the door and told him Jim was not home, he forced his way in and raped me. I was terrified and ashamed. I felt it was my fault and I never told a soul. I knew I would be blamed. That was how it was at that time, so I kept it to myself. But now with the "Me Too" movement taking hold, I want my family to know what happened to me.

Some of the more interesting and noble pursuits in my life; I was a member of a quilting group and made a number of quilts for my family, baby quilts and quilts for raffles; I participated in a homemaker group raising money for Action on Cancer; I served on The White Mountain Helping Hand Board of Directors; I served on the Election Board for eight years. And I served on the Board of Directors for the Show Low Historical Society Museum. I was also the treasurer for both the Helping Hand and Show Low Historical Society. I don't want to toot my own horn, but I am very talented in arts and crafts, home decorating, floral arranging, sewing, quilting, embroidery and cooking.

The best part of my middle years was being able to spend a lot of time with my grandkids. I had a lot of free time to spend with them and really enjoyed them so much. Anthony came after school and Tempest stayed with us often when Liz and Howard traveled. Witt and I really enjoyed having her stay with us.

One of the things I don't miss is cooking. When I was younger, I loved to cook, but now, if I don't have to, I don't. I had three girls and had to cook when they were growing up and then along came the grandkids and I cooked for them. But now it's just me and Witt and we don't do anything we don't want to do.

I miss Corrine and Louise. Janice and I got a lot closer in our later years. Witt and I used to run around with Janice and A.J. quite a bit, but not so much anymore. We met them in Heber for dinner recently. Witt used to help A.J. cut down trees in his yard, but I don't know what happened that we don't spend as much time with them. I don't know if it's us or them, but we don't do much with them anymore.

Louise Hatch, Corrine McGhee, Doris Witt, Janice Freeman

It really didn't bother me when I realized I was a senior citizen. I see a lot of people who are bothered by that, but I'm not one of them. The only thing that bothers me is all the surgeries I had to have. I don't feel old, except once in a while in the morning, when I don't get a good night's sleep. When I was 71 years old and had to have the last back surgery, it was so painful that when

I was at Liz's house in Scottsdale recovering, Howard had to help me out of my chair every time I wanted to get up. When I got home, I couldn't get out of my chair or do anything. Witt quit his job to stay home with me. It was such a change in my life. I didn't realize how much I did. I went to the post office every day, did the grocery shopping. If I needed to go other places, I did. He took over doing everything. He went to the post office and took me to the grocery store. He washed the car and put gas in it. I had never had anyone do anything for me. I always had to take care of myself. But I learned how to enjoy this new situation.

My senior years are like I envisioned them. I'm thankful I'm not alone like my mother was. Witt really doesn't like to leave home anymore and that gets to me sometimes. We could go to Phoenix and spend the weekend and do some things. There are lots of things I would enjoy doing. When Liz invites me to Scottsdale, I break my neck to do it. In 2006, Jim McCarty hosted a family reunion in Mazatlán, Mexico. He wanted to have the girls and

McCarty Family Reunion - Mazatlán, Mexico 2006

the grandkids and everyone's spouses and kids there. Tempest was the only one with kids at the time. Jim invited me and Witt. Witt didn't want to go, but I went and had a wonderful time. I was so glad I went. There were nineteen of us in all. Jim died a few months after that trip.

I would like to go to Oregon to see Witt's sister in Reedsport, but at this point in his life, Witt doesn't enjoy traveling. Earlier in our marriage, we drove often to New Mexico to visit my sister, Corrine, and my cousin, Evelyn Baldwin, and her husband, Bob Hughes. Bob and Evelyn came to Show Low to see us a few times as well. Witt and I both love New Mexico and spent time in Albuquerque, Santa Fe, Taos, Las Cruces and Espanola.

We went on several long driving trips. One was a trip to Tennessee to visit Witt's mother and sisters. They all lived in Camden, Tennessee at the time. On the way home, we stopped in Branson, Missouri. That was a really enjoyable trip.

After Witt's sister, Monita moved to Oregon, we visited her there. On that trip, we visited Mount Rushmore and Yellowstone National Park. We spent time in a place called Wall, South Dakota, home of Wall Drug. They got their start by offering free ice water. There are signs plastered all along the highways with catchy little phrases trying to get you to stop. It worked on us. We spent quite a bit of time there and it was memorable.

We went to Boston with Liz, Howard, Tempest and Victoria. Howard was doing a training session there for his software company and we all tagged along. It was in the fall and the colors were spectacular. Besides spending time seeing the sights and eating a lot in Boston, we took a few drives. On one, we ended up at the Daniel Webster Estate. Another day we went to Burlington, Vermont and wandered through a big antique store. We stopped in Hanover, New Hampshire on the way and saw Dartmouth College. Witt spotted a small sawmill in Lyme, New Hampshire where he shopped for wood for his turnings. He ordered from that sawmill for years.

I have remained active until the last few years. This last knee replacement has been keeping me down. It keeps locking up on me. Now that Witt is doing everything, I feel a little useless. I don't like people to do things for me.

People have misconceptions about getting older. Some just give up and say "I'm through. I'm not going to do anything." So many wonder what is left for them because they are old. But then I think about Imogene Brazieal. She has been a family friend for years and was the one who gave Jim and me the Chiverie. There isn't anything she won't do and I really admire her for that.

For a time, I couldn't go anywhere without Witt because of this knee. But now that it's getting better, I can go to Wal-Mart and K-Mart by myself. I can even go to Taylor to see Janice. I don't really like to drive since I'm taking Darvocet. One day, I was driving to Taylor and Kathy was in the car with me. She said I nearly ran off the road and scared the crap out of her. She made me pull over and let her drive. I don't want to drive now because I'm afraid I'm going to hurt someone. I mentioned that I wanted to drive to Scottsdale to see Liz, but Kathy's eyes got really big.

My favorite joke about the golden years is that the only thing golden is your urine. I don't really have any complaints about being old. I hope I have obtained a certain wisdom from my age. You'd be surprised how many phone calls I get from Kathy about cooking. I also get calls about cooking from Rosie, who used to clean my house.

I have become emotionally stronger as I age. I cried today talking about my mother, but I don't cry often anymore. I used to cry a lot. I think you just get older and take things in stride and realize you can't do anything about them.

I've lost lots of loved ones. I lost my mother and two sisters, my grandparents, my brother-in-law and my ex-husband. I miss them. I lost Jim's parents and I especially miss his dad.

I'm not as healthy as I would like to be, but I can't compare myself to others. It's like the old saying "Look around and you'll always find someone in a lot worse shape than you are." I never thought about how I would feel at this age and never had an expectation about it. But I don't think I'm in that bad of shape and I don't want to worry about it.

The best part about being a senior citizen is that you can do as you damn well please. And you get some discounts. I've watched a lot of senior citizens that don't care what they say to people or how they treat them. I'll never be that way. I might be old, but hopefully, I haven't lost the manners my mother taught me. She was never rude or mean as she got older. I don't intend to be that way. But I don't have to worry about being home. I can go and do what I want to do. I have no one to answer to, so I can do as I please.

The worst part about being a senior citizen is that I can't do as much. I used to be able to walk for two or three miles. I walked with Liz recently, and it wasn't that easy. And I can't drive like I used to. I used to be able to go anywhere I wanted to, but I'm not that comfortable driving anymore.

It seems like the government tries to make it easier for senior citizens. But if you try to help people more, they seem to take advantage of it. I certainly can't take advantage of those motorized chairs like the Amigo because of the stairs in my house. I could use the motorized chairs at Wal-Mart, but I won't do it until I absolutely have to use them. I have had so much trouble with my second knee replacement. It hurts most of the time, and if I'm not very careful, it locks up on me.

I like getting discounts for being a senior citizen. I can get discounts at restaurants and the movie theater. There are probably lots of perks for being a senior. Yesterday at Kohl's, it was senior day and I got fifteen percent off my purchase.

People today do not respect seniors. They don't want to be bothered. I'm sure at a senior center, you might be treated nicely and with respect, but I've never been to one.

I think I have played an important role in the lives of my grandchildren. I try to stay connected with them. I always remember their birthdays and Christmas. Even if it's just a card for their birthday, I like to send it. Tempest is the one who never misses a week that she doesn't contact me. I don't know if it's because she spent so much time with me or because she's a girl. She calls and we visit. It may just be two or three minutes or ten, but she very seldom misses a week. Most of the grandkids call me on my birthday every year and they make sure I get pictures of the great-grandkids. I feel like I really have some wonderful grandkids. Evan called recently wanting to know how to make apple strudel. He said he found a pan at a garage sale.

I think Anthony and maybe Brennon and Tempest are really thoughtful about calling and talking to me about things. I think that is a personality trait they got from me. I can't say that any of the grandkids resemble me in looks.

I hope I live for a lot longer.

Chapter Seven

Glancing Back While Looking Ahead

I am English and a Mormon. I'm proud of being English; proud that I have a country I can claim as my ancestry. Everything in Taylor revolved around the Mormon Church. We went to church, Mutual, Primary and Sunday school. I never could get up the courage to bear a testimony. We didn't always go because my mother worked on Sundays. Sometimes we didn't go. She never forced us to go to church.

Because my dad died when my sisters and I were so young, his family and my mother's helped to take care of us. They gave us food and watched over us. I was sick a lot when I was little and they finally found out it was my appendix. I had to have it removed and also my tonsils. My uncle Quill lived across the street and he gave my mother one hundred dollars to pay toward my hospital bill.

The people around town tried to take care of us. In the winter we had all these icicles and we broke them off and made ice cream in an old crank-type ice cream maker with the extended family. We went to Christmas plays with extended family. After my dad died, my dad's brother, Uncle Knut, tried to take Janice. She was just six years old and blond and cute. He and his wife weren't able to have children and he came to tell my mother they wanted to take her. My mother didn't have anything, but she wasn't willing to give up any of her girls.

Christmas, Easter and the Fourth of July were huge celebrations for us. Our birthdays were a really big deal. On my birthday, I always got a big bouquet of chrysanthemums from my grandmother Kay. They were harvested from her yard. Usually if we had a rabbit, we would kill it and fry it and have fried potatoes for my birthday dinner. Labor Day was also a big deal in Taylor. Memorial Day was a big deal. We always had to have flowers on the graves on that day. Jack Standifird and Uncle Quill were carpenters. They made sixteen-inch by sixteen-inch square boxes with glass in front for each grave. In April, we started making flowers out of crepe paper. We made roses, and if we had any wax, we would use that to make them last. This had to last a year and they didn't look that bad when it was time to do it again.

On Easter we went to the Scott ranch in Pinedale, owned by my Hancock grandparents. We had big picnics. Uncle Ralph lived at the ranch in the winter sometimes. There was no electricity. I stayed there sometimes with Gaylon. She was Uncle Ralph's daughter and a year younger than me. I got homesick every time I stayed there, and I don't remember ever eating anything good while I was there. Gaylon, Deanna and Lareen and a couple of the boys were at the Hancock reunion in Snowflake in 2012.

On the Fourth of July, Taylor had a little parade and we never missed it.

Christmas was a big deal. My mother made us wash the windows and shine them so the Christmas tree showed through the windows. One year, one of my boyfriend's brought us a pretty Christmas tree from out around Heber. We had pretty trees. We put icicles on the tree one at a time. One year we had all blue lights and one year all white lights. We didn't get very much for Christmas, but we were excited. Every year my mother hung up our old cotton socks we had to wear in the winter. We were so excited when we got up. The socks were full of candy and walnuts and oranges and some little toy. The first year my dad was gone, Burt and Reid Hatch gave each one of us a doll. We only got what we needed, like a bathrobe and pajamas and maybe a pair of shoes. We usually went to someone's house for the big Christmas meal. My mother cooked something to take along, but I remember eating at Grandma Kay's house for Christmas meals. Grandma Hancock wasn't as good a cook as Grandma Kay, but we could go to her house for Thanksgiving and sit on the south side of the house in the dining room. It was so nice and warm in that dining room. There was a big table so all of us could sit together.

We ate a lot of potatoes and gravy and green beans. We grew carrots and turnips in our garden. We ate a lot of chicken and fried rabbit once in a while. The chicken was usually baked but my mother could make a mean fried chicken. We had beef roast and lamb and pinto beans. We didn't have a refrigerator or freezer, so milk and other things like that had to be stored outside in the snow. My mother would get a side of pork or beef and hang it on the outside of the house. She would go outside with a knife and cut off enough for a meal. I don't remember what we did with things like that in the summer. I don't think we had much around that needed to be refrigerated. We didn't have an icebox because it wasn't that easy to get a block of ice in Taylor.

It is important to me to maintain a strong identity with my ethnic and cultural heritage. My entire family is Mormon. That's how they got to the United States and I think that is why they joined the Mormon Church. It allowed them to leave England. They were working themselves to the bone every day and still starving. The jobs were unbelievable and they would have done anything to leave there. A typical Mormon worship service would have been Sunday school first and then the church service began after that. It started at nine o'clock and we would be home by around two. We were gone for a long time. When we got back to the house, it was cold. We had Mutual on Tuesday nights. That's where we learned to square dance and round dance. We had parties. We knew all the kids in town and had lots of fun together. In the summer we had cookouts and picnics. Once we went to Daggs Reservoir for a cookout and Margie and I took off our clothes and went swimming. When we got out of the water, it took us forever to find our clothes. I'll never forget that, because we were starting to panic and thought someone had run off with them.

I'm very proud to belong to my family. They are good people. I'm proud to be English. Churchill was a good leader and he worked with U.S. President Roosevelt to end World War II. I admire Churchill. I can't imagine what would have happened if we hadn't been allies with England. I would love to go to England. The closest I've been is landing in London on our way back from Greece.

My mother was not fond of Mexicans. A lot of Mexicans came into the Grill Café where she worked. She didn't talk a lot about them. When I was sixteen, a group of black people stopped by the café and Burt Hatch wouldn't let them come in. There was a little window on the south side of the door facing east, and they had to order there and receive their food there. It was embarrassing, but everyone did it. When we went to the movies in McNary, the black people had to sit up in the balcony away from the rest of us who sat on the lower floors.

I don't think much about interracial marriage. I have grandsons that are Mexican and Tempest's kids are Mexican. There are a lot of Hancock's that married blacks. I thought it was pretty neat when I saw them at the Hancock reunion in 2012.

The Mormons celebrate the 24th of July. It's when the Mormons arrived in the Salt Lake Valley in 1847. Every year, my sisters and I waited outside our house to see Apache natives arriving from Whiteriver in covered wagons for the parade. We were so fascinated to see them. They came mostly for the rodeo.

When I was a child, I heard about people being attacked and killed by Apache natives around Show Low. A lot of people hid when they came around. This happened before I was born. I assume it was over and done with by the time I was a kid.

My cousin, Anna Lou Ozment, married an African American from Holbrook or Winslow. Since then, her daughter, Stellie married an African American as well. One of Lana's girls, Leah, lived with a black man for a while and had a couple of kids. People in Taylor were prejudiced when I was growing up. They still are. Their parents teach it to them. There is no other way to say it. I never taught my kids to be prejudiced. People need to realize it's not the right thing to do, but I think it's hard not to have some prejudices.

Be proud of your ethnic group no matter what it might be. I'd like to know more about my heritage. I'd like to visit the places in England where my ancestors lived.

I'd like to visit New York, Washington D.C., and the thirteen colonies. I would like to see some of that country and some of those monuments. I'd like to see Gettysburg and other Civil War places.

I hope I have made peace with everyone important in my life. I don't have any nagging thoughts about that.

I need to try to learn to control my temper. I lost my temper a lot with my first husband because he was so domineering. Maybe it was a good thing I did that, because it made me realize that I did need to try to control it.

People need to be made to feel important. It's more important to plan for the future than to live in the present. I'm concerned that at my funeral my children will say I was a witch.

Doris suffered a devastating stroke on December 27, 2022. The stroke left her unable to speak or swallow. She died at her daughter Kathy's home on January 1, 2023. She was 88 years old. Her children did not say she was a witch at her celebration of life.

Obituary

Doris Kay Witt left us on New Year's Day, 2023, sort of surrounded by her loving family. In keeping with her tenacious nature, she waited until the four-minute mid-day shift change, while one family member was coming down the stairs and another was going up, to quietly make her exit. She will be missed by all who knew her, especially her husband, children, grandchildren, great-grandchildren, nieces, nephews and friends.

Doris was born on October 25, 1934 to Afton Hancock Kay and John Henry Kay in Taylor, Arizona. As the fourth born, she was the baby of a family of four girls that included Louise (Jay) Hatch, Corrine (Bobby) McGhee, and Janice (AJ) Freeman, with whom she spent many hours avoiding, or finding, trouble depending on who you asked. Her father died when she was four years old and she and her sisters were raised by a single mother in 1940s Taylor, Arizona.

In 1952, while working at The Grill Café in Snowflake, Arizona, Doris met Jim McCarty. They married in 1953 and had three daughters, Liz (Howard Jones) McCarty, Victoria McCarty, and Kathy (Mike) Fish. Doris spent years engulfed in sewing, cooking, boating, water skiing, camping, PTA meetings, private flute and clarinet lessons, sports matches, speech tournaments, school plays, band camp, working polls (voting polls), designing flower arrangements, gardening, bookkeeping, driving garbage and dump trucks, painting artistically and fiercely defending her daughters.

Doris and Jim divorced in 1977, after which she learned to snow ski, and then bought a home in Paradise Valley so she could keep herself occupied and live in a warmer climate in winter. During this period, she became a dental assistant, and also spent time in Safford, Arizona learning everything one might want to know, or not, about calves and running a feed lot, finally returning to sanity and Show Low full time in the early 1980s.

In 1984 she married her paperboy, Larry "Witt" Witt, whom she met when she and Jim were living in Ash Fork, AZ in the early 1950s and he was delivering their newspaper. Don't read anything into that. It was over thirty years later, Witt was living in Show Low at the time, and he was no longer employed as a paperboy.

Along with Witt, came two sons, Doug (Julie) Witt and Mike Witt. Doris and Witt embarked on a life of sharing children, grandchildren, great- grandchildren and logging, among other things, but the logging stands out as an interesting way to spend a day. Witt logged in Arizona and many other places, with Doris by his side, until they decided to stay home, at which time Witt began delivering materials for Perkins Cinders and Doris volunteered with the Show Low Historical Society at the Show Low Museum until she and Witt retired. Doris and Witt were married for 38 glorious years before they went their separate ways, because, hey, this isn't Egypt.

Doris loved to read, garden, clean, (yeah, we know), paint, embroider, hike and cook. She excelled at them all. In her early 40's, Doris developed arthritis, which became debilitating over the years. She proved to be a tough old bird and carried around more metal than Ironman. Eventually it curbed her active lifestyle but she continued to laugh and light up a room. She filled her homes with her sparkling laughter and beautiful smile, always welcoming to all. Doris was fun, beautiful, determined, resilient, and she was a sweetheart. She is forever in our hearts and we will miss her for the rest of our lives.

Doris was preceded in death by her father, mother, sisters and the father of her children. She leaves behind her husband, daughters, sons, sons-in-law, daughter-in-law, nine grandchildren; Alexander (Crystal) Ellerbe, Trevor Fish,

Tempest Jones, Anthony (Amanda) Ellerbe, Evan (Cara) Fish, Brennon (Danica) Fish, April (Jason) Carl, Jeremy (Erica) Witt, and Maryann Witt, and 23 great-grandchildren. The service was private.

Pickle Queen Recipes

My sisters and I enjoy fond memories of our mother's cooking. She was a stay-at-home mom and cooked dinner almost every night. Her cooking style was simple but delicious. She certainly had the knowledge to make inexpensive meats taste like a million dollars. The low and slow method was something she mastered long before the slow cooker or crockpot became a thing.

We never knew what would be waiting for us when we arrived home from school. Cookies, cakes, pies, brownies; it was never-ending and always good. Friends and cousins loved to come home with us because they knew they would get to enjoy those homemade treats as well.

In June of 2022, we spent time with our mom, picking her brain about our favorites and going through her written recipes. What follows is that collection of mouth-watering memories.

When we were growing up, mom used Crisco, margarine and Miracle Whip. We decided to keep the recipes as she had prepared them. When we cook them now, we use olive or canola oil, butter and mayonnaise. Do as you wish.

Some of the recipes might have been taken from a newspaper or magazine. We are not giving credit to mom for anything but cooking good food no matter where the recipe originated.

A few of the recipes came from our grandmothers, other relatives and friends. Those are noted next to the recipe.

Appetizers and Snacks

Chex Snack Mix

3 cups corn Chex cereal
3 cups rice Chex cereal
3 cups wheat Chex cereal
1 cup mixed nuts
1 cup bite size pretzels
1 cup garlic flavor bite size bagel chips
6 tablespoons butter or margarine
2 tablespoons Worchester Sauce
1 ½ teaspoon Lawry's Seasoned Salt
¾ teaspoon garlic powder
½ teaspoon onion powder

In large bowl mix cereals, nuts, pretzels and bagel chips. Melt butter or margarine and add Worchester Sauce, Lawry's, garlic and onion powder. Pour over cereal mixture and mix gently. Spread onto baking sheets and bake for 30 minutes in 300° oven, stirring every 10 minutes. Spread on paper towels to cool. Store in air-tight container.

Chinese Egg Rolls

A Chinese family lived in Show Low. They owned a grocery store. Eventually, one of the sons opened a Chinese restaurant. He was a good friend of our parents and taught mom to make these egg rolls.

2 cups carrot, finely chopped
2 cups celery, finely chopped
1 cup bean sprouts, finely chopped
3 scallions, thinly sliced
2 ½ teaspoons salt
1 teaspoon pepper
2 tablespoons soy sauce
3 cups roast pork, shredded or diced
3 cups cooked chicken, shredded or diced
2 cups raw shrimp, finely chopped
2 packages egg roll wrappers (about 48 pieces)
1 egg (beaten)
Peanut or vegetable oil, for frying

Place all of the vegetables, meat and shrimp in a large bowl. Add the salt, pepper and soy sauce. Toss everything together. To wrap the egg rolls, take a small fistful of filling, squeeze it a little in your hand until it is compressed together, and place it on the wrapper. The wrapping method is similar to that of a burrito. Just add a thin layer of egg to make sure it stays sealed. Line them up on a lightly floured surface and continue assembling until you run out of ingredients.

In a small pot, heat oil to 325°. You don't need too much—just enough to submerge the egg rolls. Carefully place a couple egg rolls into the oil and fry them for about 5 minutes until golden brown. Keep them moving in the oil to make sure they fry evenly. Cool slightly. Freeze leftovers in freezer bags and reheat them in the oven at 350°, until crispy.

Pitty Pats

Mom found this recipe when we were kids and it quickly became a favorite. It might have been published in the Arizona Republic. I recently found it in NYT Cooking. It is called Sausage Balls and is credited to Julia Reed.

4 ½ cups Bisquick® baking mix
15 ounces cheddar cheese, grated
24 ounces Jimmy Dean pork sausage, hot or mild
3/4 cup water

Heat oven to 350°. Combine ingredients like meat loaf. Roll into small balls and bake on cookie sheet for 20 to 25 minutes; or bake 15 minutes and freeze then bake 15 minutes more without thawing.

Sweet and Sour Meatballs

Our parents had big Christmas parties for the employees. This was always on the menu.

2 pounds fully cooked beef, lamb or pork meatballs
1 cup grape jelly
1 cup bar-be-que sauce

Place grape jelly and bar-be-que sauce in crock pot large enough to hold meatballs. Heat on high until mixture comes together when stirred. Add meatballs, cover and reduce to low.

Pimento Cheese

This was a cult favorite in our family. We loved it on white bread or stuffed in celery. Our mom used Miracle Whip in a lot of things. Feel free to swap it out with mayonnaise.

2 cups cheddar cheese, grated
¾ cup Miracle Whip
1 (4 ounce) jar diced pimento, drained

Mix all ingredients until thoroughly combined.

Roast Beef Sandwich Filling

We spent countless weekends and summers camping and boating. Mom made almost all of the food for those outings at home. This was and still is, a favorite. She used an old cast iron meat grinder. You can use a food processor. The amounts of the ingredients will depend on how much roast beef on hand.

Left over beef roast, chopped
Onion, roughly chopped
Sweet pickles, roughly chopped
Miracle Whip to taste

Place roast beef, onion and sweet pickles in food processor. Pulse until mixture reaches your preferred texture. Remove from processor into bowl and add Miracle Whip to taste.

Main Dishes

Beef Stew

This is the recipe Grandma Kay used when she worked at The Grill Café.

2 pounds stew meat or sirloin steak
1 teaspoon salt
1 teaspoon pepper
Garlic salt to taste
2 tablespoons Crisco
2 celery ribs, sliced
1 onion, chopped
3 carrots, chopped
3 potatoes, chopped
1 8-ounce can tomato sauce or 1 14½-ounce can peeled tomatoes

 Season meat with salt, pepper, and garlic salt. In large pot or Dutch oven, brown meat in Crisco on medium heat. Add celery, carrots, onions, and potatoes. Add tomato sauce or peeled tomatoes and enough water to cover contents of pan. Simmer for 2 hours.

Beer Stew

1 pound beef stew meat
1 can or bottle beer
26-ounce can Ranch Style Beans

Place everything in a slow cooker. Cook until liquid reduces, six to eight hours on high.

Bobby McGhee's Green Chili and Rice

Our uncle Bobby McGhee used to stay with us in Show Low when he worked at the sawmill in McNary. Mom made this once and he loved it so much, she made if for him once a week.

2 pounds roast beef, sliced
1 can diced green chilies
1 medium onion, chopped
1 large tomato, chopped
1 14½-ounce can beef broth
Cooked rice

Simmer roast beef and vegetables in beef broth for one hour. Serve over hot rice.

Carne Asada

1 12-ounce can beer
Salt
Dried Mexican oregano
Pinch of pepper
Dash of garlic salt
1 3-to 4-pound chuck roast

Salsa
1 cup fresh green chilies
1 large ripe tomato, finely chopped reserving juices
½ medium white onion, chopped
3 green onions, finely chopped
Cilantro leaves, chopped
Yellow peppers to taste, finely chopped
Salt and pepper to taste

Pour beer into casserole dish. Add enough salt to lend a gritty feel to beer and produce a foaming effect. Add oregano, crumbling the whole leaves thoroughly. Use enough that a layer covers the beer. Add pepper and garlic salt.

Remove large fatty parts from meat. Cut meat into pieces about 2 x 3 inches. Butterfly the pieces by cutting each almost in half and holding it open, place in marinade. Marinate at least ten minutes, or overnight. Grill to desired doneness and serve with salsa.

Roast green chilies in oven or on bar-be-cue until blistered and charred in places. Place in paper bag to sweat. When cool enough, remove skins and discard. Chop into small pieces. In large bowl mix green chilies with tomato and juice from tomato. Add both onions, cilantro, and yellow peppers. Add salt and pepper to taste.

Chicken Fried Steak

2 pounds round or cube steak, tenderized
Lawry's Seasoned Salt
Pepper
Flour
Equal parts Crisco and margarine

Liberally season steak with Lawry's Seasoned Salt and pepper.
Dredge in flour. Melt Crisco and margarine in large skillet on
medium. Cook steaks to desired doneness.

Chili Rellenos

4 eggs, separated
4 tablespoons flour
3/4 cup milk
1 pound Monterey Jack cheese, shredded
1 pound longhorn cheese, shredded
20 ounces whole green chilies
La Victoria salsa

Heat oven to 350°. Beat egg yolks and whites separately, then together with flour and milk. Mix cheeses together. Oil 9-inch x 13-inch casserole. Layer green chilies and cheeses. Pour egg mixture over. Bake 45 minutes. Pour salsa over for last 10 minutes of baking.

Fried Chicken

We got to eat this fried chicken once a week. It was served with mashed potatoes and white gravy mom made using the drippings from the chicken. It was simple and simply delicious.

1 fryer chicken, cut up
Lawry's Seasoned Salt
Pepper
½ cup flour
Equal parts Crisco and margarine

Season chicken liberally with Lawry's Seasoned Salt and pepper. Place flour in clean paper bag. Drop chicken in bag and shake bag until chicken is covered in flour. Heat Crisco and margarine in a large skillet. Fry chicken until crisp and tender and internal temperature registers 165°.

Green Chili Stew

5 pounds round steak, cubed
5 tablespoons bacon fat
1 cup + 2 tablespoons onion, diced
3 cloves garlic, minced
48 ounces stewed tomatoes, chopped
40 ounces chopped green chilies
1 ½ teaspoon coarse ground red chili powder
1 teaspoon black pepper
8 medium potatoes, cubed
8 cups water

Brown meat in bacon fat. Add onions and garlic and cook until golden. Add remaining ingredients and simmer 1 to 2 hours. Serves 15 to 20.

Ground Beef Tacos

Dad loved to put French's yellow mustard on the left-over tacos and eat them for breakfast, cold.

1 pound ground beef
1 pound cheddar cheese, grated
1 dozen corn tortillas
Crisco
Iceberg lettuce, chopped
Tomato, chopped
Onion, chopped

Cook ground beef until crispy. Fry tortillas one at a time in Criso on medium-high until crisp. Fold over and drain on paper towel. Fill each tortilla with meat, cheese, lettuce, tomato and onion.

Oven Shrimp

4 tablespoons margarine
2 pounds medium shrimp, peeled and cleaned
Salt and pepper
4 cloves garlic, minced

Heat oven to 450°. Melt margarine in baking sheet in oven.
Season shrimp with salt and pepper. Toss garlic with shrimp.
Remove pan from oven and add shrimp and garlic. Place in oven
and cook for three to four minutes until shrimp are pink.

Red Chili Enchiladas

1 pound ground beef
2 onions, chopped, divided
Equal parts flour and red chili powder
1 8-ounce can tomato sauce
Pace Salsa
Cheddar cheese, grated
Corn tortillas

Heat oven to 350°. Brown ground beef and add one onion. Cook until beef is no longer pink. Add flour and red chili powder and cook for 2 minutes. Add tomato sauce and ½ cup water and simmer five minutes. Warm corn tortillas in oven. Divide meat mixture among tortillas. Add cheese and chopped raw onion. Roll each tortilla and place in baking dish. Cover with any remaining sauce from pan and Pace Salsa and cheese. Bake for 30 minutes.

Salmon Cakes

This was mom's trick to get us to eat fish other than Van de Kamp's Frozen Fish Sticks.

1 14.75 ounce can salmon
1 egg
¼ cup onion, chopped
½ cup seasoned Italian bread crumbs
½ teaspoon salt
½ teaspoon pepper
1 tablespoon Crisco
1 tablespoon margarine

Mix salmon, egg, onion and bread crumbs with salt and pepper. Form into ½-inch thick patties. Melt Crisco and margarine in large skillet. Fry salmon patties for 2 minutes on each side.

Short Ribs

This was an all-time favorite dish. Mom browned the ribs using no fat or oil. They came out of the oven falling off the bone.

4 pounds bone-in short ribs
Johnny's Seasoning Salt

Heat oven to 250°. Season short ribs liberally with Johnny's Seasoning Salt. Brown on all sides in Dutch oven. Cover Dutch oven and slip into oven for six hours.

Sour Cream Enchiladas

2 tablespoons margarine
1 onion, chopped
1 pint sour cream
2 cans cream of chicken soup
1 ½ cans diced green chilies
1 small chicken, cooked and shredded
2 dozen corn tortillas
Crisco
1 pound cheddar cheese, grated
1 15-ounce can or jar of green chili enchilada sauce
1 15-ounce can or jar of red chili enchilada sauce

Heat oven to 350°. Melt margarine in small skillet. Add half of the onion and cook until soft. Transfer to a large bowl and add sour cream, cream of chicken soup, green chilies and chicken. Soften tortillas in melted Crisco. Fill each with chicken mixture, raw onions and cheese. Lay side-by-side in 9-inch by 13-inch pan. Cover with enchilada sauces and any remaining cheese. Bake until bubbling and cheese is melted, approximately 30 minutes.

Steak Picante

2 pounds round or cube steak, tenderized
Lawry's Seasoned Salt
½ cup flour
Crisco or neutral cooking oil
1 small onion, diced
1 large tomato, diced
1 can diced green chilies
½ teaspoon liquid smoke

Season round steak with Lawry's and dredge steak in flour. Melt
Crisco or heat oil in large skillet on medium high and brown
steak on both sides. Reduce heat to medium low and add onion
and liquid smoke. Simmer for 30 minutes. Remove lid and add
tomatoes and green chilies. Simmer for 5 minutes.

Stuffed Peppers and Tomatoes

5 small green peppers
5 large tomatoes
1 medium onion, chopped
3 tablespoons oil
½ pounds each ground pork and beef
1 cup cooked rice
1 teaspoon salt
½ teaspoon pepper
1 egg, beaten
2 small cans tomato sauce

Wash peppers and tomatoes, cut off tops, remove seeds and scrape insides with spoon. Brown ground meat and onion in oil. Remove to a bowl and add rice, salt, pepper and egg. Mix well. Fill peppers and tomatoes just shy of full with meat mixture. Place peppers and tomatoes in deep pot. Gently pour tomato sauce and enough water to cover. Simmer, covered for 1 hour or until tender.

Side Dishes and Salads

Cherry Delight (Afton Kay)

Afton Kay was mom's mother

1 cup sugar
3 ½ cups hot water
2 small packages cherry Jell-O
1 16-ounce can crushed pineapple
2 ½ cups cooked, cooled white rice
1 large size Cool Whip
1 cup walnuts, chopped
1 cup maraschino cherries, chopped

Dissolve sugar and Jell-O in hot water. Add pineapple and rice. Stir well. Cool until almost set and add Cool Whip, nuts, and maraschino cherries. Chill until set.

Cornbread Stuffing

Cornbread
1 cup yellow cornmeal
1 cup all-purpose flour
1 teaspoon salt
1 1/3 tablespoons double-acting baking powder
1 egg
1 cup milk
4 tablespoon butter, melted

Stuffing
5 cups crumbled yellow cornbread
1 pound sausage meat
2 cups chopped onion
1 ½ chopped celery stalks
2 cups lightly pressed fresh white bread crumbs
2 eggs, lightly beaten
Salt and pepper
2 to 3 tablespoons dried sage
½ cup (4 ounces) butter, melted

Heat oven to 400°. Combine cornmeal, flour, salt, and baking powder. Whisk egg, milk, and butter and add to dry ingredients. Beat together for one minute. Bake 20 minutes in a greased 8-inch square pan. Crumble when cool.

Heat oven to 375°. Break up the sausage meat; sauté in a skillet for several minutes, until gray. Use a slotted spoon to transfer sausage to a large mixing bowl, leaving fat in pan. Using same pan, sauté onions five to six minutes or until tender but not brown, add celery and sauté 2 minutes. Add the sauteed vegetables to the sausage, along with the cornbread, white bread crumbs and eggs. Season nicely to taste, exaggerating a bit with the sage. Fold in the melted butter. Cook in buttered 9-x 13-inch pan to desired doneness. Makes about 2 ½ quarts stuffing.

Green Beans with Cheese

This is another recipe mom cooked often and it was always on the Thanksgiving table.

3 tablespoons butter, melted
2 tablespoons flour
1 teaspoon salt
¼ teaspoon pepper
1 teaspoon sugar
½ teaspoon onion, grated
1 cup sour cream
24 ounces canned French Cut green beans, drained
½ cup fresh bread crumbs
½ pound cheddar cheese

Combine 2 tablespoons butter and flour. Cook gently. Remove from heat. Stir in salt, pepper, sugar, onion, and sour cream. Fold in beans and place in shallow 2-quart casserole. Cover with cheese and bread crumbs mixed with remaining tablespoon of butter. Place in 350° oven and bake for 30 minutes.

Homemade Noodles

4 egg yolks
1 whole egg
2 teaspoons salt
¼ cup heavy cream
2 cups flour (more or less)

Beat egg yolks, whole egg, salt, and cream until smooth. Add
flour until the mixture is very, very dry. Roll into a ball. Divide
ball in two pieces. Working with one half at a time, roll out very
thinly on floured board. Fold dough as if folding a dishtowel.
Cut into thin strips and return to bowl. When all noodles are in
bowl, toss them with 2 tablespoons flour. Cook noodles in
boiling stew for 15 minutes.

Japanese Salad

2 packages chicken flavored ramen noodles and flavor packets
1 head cabbage – chopped
1 or 2 cans chicken (or chicken breast), cut up
4 tablespoons almonds, slivered
4 green onions, sliced

Dressing
6 tablespoons vinegar
2 tablespoons sugar
1 teaspoon salt
1 teaspoon pepper
1 teaspoon Accent
Ramen flavor packets
¾ cup oil

Crush the ramen noodles in a large serving bowl. Mix remaining ingredients together with noodles.

Place vinegar, sugar, salt, pepper, Accent, and Ramen flavor packets together in medium bowl until sugar is dissolved. Slowly add oil, whisking constantly. Pour dressing over cabbage mixture and toss well. Let cool a couple of hours.

Orange Jell-O Salad

1 16 oz. carton large curd cottage cheese
1 small carton Cool Whip
1 can mandarin orange slices, drained
1 can pineapple tidbits, drained
2 cups small marshmallows
1 3 oz. package orange Jell-O

Stir all ingredients except Jell-O together and mix well. Sprinkle dry Jell-O over and mix well. Chill before serving.

Peach Salad

Canned Peach Halves (one half per serving)
Miracle Whip (2 teaspoons per serving)
Cheddar Cheese, grated (3 teaspoons per serving)

Place one peach half on salad plate. Fill with Miracle Whip. Top with cheese.

Potato Salad

5 medium russet potatoes
5 eggs, hard boiled, chopped
1 medium yellow onion, chopped
4 Clausen dill pickles, chopped
½ large can whole black olives, chopped
1 cup Miracle Whip
2 tablespoon yellow mustard
Salt to taste
Pepper galore

Boil potatoes whole then peel and dice to 2-inch cubes. Place potatoes in a large bowl and add eggs, onion, pickles, and olives. Mix Miracle Whip and mustard together in small bowl and then mix into other ingredients. Add salt and pepper.

Tomato Pie

1 blind baked pie crust
4 plum tomatoes, sliced 1/8-inch thick
Salt and pepper
Chives, sliced
Basil, diced
1 cup mayonnaise
1 cup sharp cheddar cheese, grated
8 slices bacon, diced and cooked

Heat oven to 350°. Layer tomatoes with salt, pepper, chives, and basil in blind baked crust. Mix mayonnaise and cheese; spread over tomatoes. Bake for 20 minutes. Top with crumbled bacon and bake an additional 10 minutes.

Bread

Dad's Refrigerator Rolls

3 cups hot water
¼ pound butter
3 packages yeast
¾ cup sugar
2 teaspoons salt
3 eggs, beaten
7 cups flour
2 tablespoons Crisco
2 tablespoons butter, melted

Mix hot water and butter together. When butter is melted, add yeast. Blend all together, then add sugar, salt, eggs and flour. Mix and let rise one hour until doubled in bulk. Roll dough and cut with biscuit cutter. Melt Crisco in pan. Turn rolls in Crisco. Let rise. Bake at 375° for about 15 minutes or until brown. Brush tops with melted butter when done.

Cinnamon rolls can also be made with this dough. Roll out thin, spread with melted butter. Sprinkle with brown sugar and cinnamon. Roll up and cut. Lay in greased pan and let rise, then bake. Frost while still warm or after they are cool.

Mexican Corn Bread

2 eggs, beaten
½ cup oil
1 cup buttermilk
1 15.25-ounce can creamed corn
1 cup corn meal
1 cup flour
3 teaspoons baking powder
1 teaspoon salt
10 ounces cheddar cheese, grated
1 4-ounce can diced green chilies

Grease a 9-inch by 13-inch pan. Heat oven to 350°. Mix eggs, oil, buttermilk and creamed corn. Mix corn meal, flour, baking powder and salt. Pour egg mixture over corn meal mixture and mix lightly. Pour half of batter into pan. Add half of cheese and half of chilies. Pour in remaining batter and top with remaining cheese and chilies. Bake for 1 hour.

Sour Dough Bread

Do not screw lid tightly on starter. Leave loose. It must breathe.

Step 1:
Add to starter (a.m.)
1 cup flour
½ cup sugar
1 cup warm water
3 heaping tablespoons instant potato flakes

Stir and leave uncovered at room temperature all day. Stir occasionally.

Step 2:
Remove 1 cup starter from bowl. Return rest of starter to the refrigerator. Save the left-over starter 3-7 days, then repeat Step 1.

Add to 1 cup starter:
1/3 cup sugar
1 ½ cup warm water
½ cup oil
1 tablespoon salt
1 package yeast
5 ½ cups flour

Mix together. Place dough in well buttered bowl. Turn to butter top. Cover. Let rise all night.

Step 3:
Place dough on floured board. Divide into 3 sections. Knead 8-10 times. Place in buttered pans. Cover with buttered waxed paper. Let rise all day.

Step 4:
Bake at 350° for 30 minutes for loaves. Remove from oven onto cooling racks. Butter tops of bread.

Makes 3 loaves. You can take one section and make a dozen rolls if you choose.

Note: You must "feed" your starter every 3 -7 days. Do step 1 and return starter to refrigerator if you don't want to make the bread.

Texas Toast

Thickly sliced white bread
Garlic Salt
Pan drippings from chicken fried steak
Margarine

Melt margarine with pan drippings. Add garlic salt. Place bread slices in pan and turn to coat. Cook until toasted on one side and turn over to finish toasting on other side.

Gravy and Sauces

Shrimp Sauce (Afton Kay)

2 cups catsup
1 small onion, diced
1 celery stalk, diced

Mix all and serve with cooked, peeled and chilled shrimp.

Spanish Sauce (Afton Kay)

2 or 3 springs celery, chopped
1 bell pepper, chopped
2 medium onions, chopped
1 can tomatoes
1 cup chili hot sauce
1 teaspoon salt
1 teaspoon sugar

Mix all ingredients together. Use for tacos and enchiladas.

White Gravy

Pan drippings
Margarine
½ cup flour
2 cups milk

Melt enough butter with pan drippings to equal one-half cup.
Add flour and cook for three minutes. Add milk and whisk until
smooth and bubbly.

Pickles and Relish

Dill Pickles

4 1-quart wide-mouth canning jars with lids
2 quarts water
1 quart white vinegar
1 scant cup salt
Pickling cucumbers
Dill flowers

Bring all ingredients to a boil.

Pack cucumbers in bottle with flower of dill, 1 ½ bud garlic, and one hot red chili pepper. Pour water vinegar mixture over and seal.

Relish

Mom made this using a cast iron grinder. You can use a food processor.

Grind 4 quarts cucumbers and 2 quarts onions. Soak cucumbers and onions for 1 hour in water salted to taste. Drain water and add:

3 cups sugar
1 quart vinegar
2 tablespoons mustard seed
2 teaspoons celery seed
2 teaspoons pepper

Boil for 30 minutes. Add chili flakes if desired. Add turmeric and seal hot.

Tangy Mixed Pickles

18 1-pint canning jars and caps
4 pounds long, thin cucumbers, cut into ¼-inch slices
3 large sweet green peppers, cut into 1-inch chunks
3 large sweet red peppers, cut into 1-inch chunks
1 ½ pounds small onions, sliced ¼-inch thick
1 bunch celery, cut into ¾-inch pieces
1 small head cauliflower, broken into flowerets
12 cups cider vinegar
6 cups sugar
1/3 cup turmeric
¼ cup salt
1 teaspoon crushed red peppers (optional)

Prepare jars and caps for processing.

In large bowl, combine cucumbers, peppers, onions, celery, and cauliflower; set aside. In 5-quart Dutch oven over high heat, heat vinegar, sugar, turmeric, salt, crushed red pepper and 6 cups water to boiling, stirring occasionally. Reduce heat to low; keep liquid simmering.

Pack vegetable mixture tightly into hot jar to within ½-inch of the top of jar. Ladle liquid over vegetables, leaving ¼-inch space from the top of jar. Close jars as manufacturer directs. Process in boiling water bath for 15 minutes. Cool jars and test for airtight seal. Store unopened pickles in cool, dry place to use within one year. Makes 18 pints.

Sweet Things

Grandma Kay's Pie Crust (Afton Kay)

Our grandma Kay was the best pie maker in Navajo County back in the day. She taught mom to make those pies and we all loved them. This recipe makes two crusts.

3 cups flour (do not sift)
3 teaspoons sugar
1 teaspoon salt
1 1/4 cups Crisco (can use half butter)
2/3 cup ice water (approximately – use enough to hold dough together)

Mix dry ingredients and cut in Crisco and butter, if using. Add water and mix just until it forms a ball. Refrigerate for at least one hour and up to three days. Can be frozen.

Apple Strudel

This is not the typical strudel. Mom got the recipe from Virginia Linde, a good friend. Virginia was visiting from Phoenix one weekend when my dad brought home a lot of Golden Delicious apples from an orchard he owned in Shumway, Arizona.

One recipe Grandma Kay's pie crust
5 Golden Delicious apples, peeled and thinly sliced
1¼ cup sugar
3 teaspoons flour
1 tablespoon cinnamon
Juice of one lemon
Butter

Glaze
1 cup confectioner's sugar
2 tablespoons butter
½ teaspoon vanilla
2 – 4 tablespoons milk

This strudel should be made in a 12-inch pizza pan with ½-inch sides.

Heat oven to 375°. Mix apples with sugar, flour, cinnamon and lemon juice. Let sit for at least 10 minutes while you prepare the crust. Roll out one half of the pie crust to fit a 12-inch x ½ inch round pizza pan. Fit crust into pan. Fill pan with apple mixture and dot with butter. Roll out the remaining dough and cover the apples. Press the edges together, trim the excess, then crimp the edges with your fingers. Using a sharp knife, cut three or four steam vents in the top of the crust in a decorative pattern. Bake for one hour. Glaze while strudel is hot.

Cream butter and confectioner's sugar. Add vanilla. Mix in milk one tablespoon at a time until it reaches the consistency of a light glaze.

Butterscotch Pie (Afton Kay)

½ recipe Grandma Kay's Pie Crust
1 box butterscotch pudding
½ box vanilla pudding
2 cups milk
¼ cup brown sugar
3 egg yolks, beaten

Meringue
3 egg whites
¼ teaspoon cream of tartar
6 tablespoons sugar

Preheat oven to 425°. On a lightly floured surface, roll dough to a 1/8-in.-thick circle; transfer to a 9-in. pie plate. Trim to ½ inch beyond rim of plate; flute edge. Refrigerate 30 minutes.

Line crust with a double thickness of foil. Fill with pie weights, dried beans or uncooked rice. Bake on a lower oven rack until edge is light golden brown, 15-20 minutes. Remove foil and weights; bake until bottom is golden brown, 3-6 minutes longer. Cool on a wire rack. Reduce oven setting to 350°.

In a saucepan, over medium-high heat, cook puddings with milk and brown sugar until thickened and bubbly. Reduce heat; cook and stir 2 minutes longer. Remove from the heat. Stir about 1 cup hot filling into egg yolks; return all to pan, stirring constantly. Bring to a gentle boil; cook and stir for 2 minutes longer. Remove from the heat. Pour into crust.

For meringue, beat egg whites and cream of tartar in a small bowl on medium speed until soft peaks form. Gradually beat in sugar, about 1 tablespoon at a time, on high until stiff glossy peaks form and sugar is dissolved. Spread evenly over hot filling, sealing edge to crust.

Bake until meringue is golden brown, 12-15 minutes. Cool on a wire rack for 1 hour. Refrigerate at least 3 hours before serving. Refrigerate leftovers.

Cherry Pie (Afton Kay)

One recipe Grandma Kay's pie crust
1 cup sugar
3 tablespoons corn starch
¼ teaspoon salt
½ teaspoon cinnamon
1 tablespoon lemon juice
2 pounds sweet cherries, pitted
2 tablespoons milk
1 tablespoon white sugar

Heat oven to 425°. Position rack in lower third of oven. In a large bowl toss together sugar, corn starch, salt, cinnamon and lemon juice. Add cherries and stir gently. Line a 9-inch pie dish with one crust. Pour filling into the prepared pie dish. Cover with remaining crust; press and flute the edges to seal. Cut a few steam vents on top, brush with milk, and sprinkle with sugar. Bake 10 minutes and reduce oven to 350°. Bake until golden brown, about 55 to 60 minutes.

Pineapple Pie (Afton Kay)

One recipe Grandma Kay's pie crust
1 20-ounce can crushed pineapple
¾ cup sugar
½ teaspoon salt
2 tablespoons corn starch
3 tablespoons water
2 tablespoons milk
1 tablespoon white sugar

Heat oven to 425°. Bring pineapple, sugar and salt to boil. Dissolve corn starch in water and add to pineapple mixture. Continue cooking until thickened. Line a 9-inch pie dish with one crust. Pour filling into the prepared pie dish. Cover with remaining crust; press and flute the edges to seal. Cut a few steam vents on top, brush with milk, and sprinkle with sugar. Bake until golden brown, about 35 minutes. Serve chilled or at room temperature.

Peach Cobbler (Jane Dalton)

Jane Dalton was a friend of mom. She lived in Phoenix but visited often.

1 stick butter
1 29-ounce can peaches (or same amount of fresh peaches, sliced)
1 cup sugar plus more for sprinkling
1 cup flour
½ teaspoon salt
2 teaspoon baking powder
1 cup milk

Heat oven to 350°. Melt butter in cobbler pan. Pour peaches over melted butter. Mix 1 cup sugar, flour, salt, and baking powder. Add milk. Mix well and pour over peaches and butter. Sprinkle liberally with sugar. Bake for 30 to 45 minutes.

Date Pin Wheels (Stormi Langston)

Stormi was a friend of mom. She lived in Show Low for years.

1 cup sugar
1 cup brown sugar, packed
1 cup Crisco
2 to 3 eggs, beaten
1 teaspoon vanilla
4 cups flour
1 teaspoon soda
½ teaspoon salt

Filling
16 ounces dates, sliced
1 cup nuts, chopped
½ cup sugar
½ cup water

Heat oven to 350°. In a large bowl cream sugars and Crisco. Add beaten eggs and vanilla. In a medium bowl mix flour, soda, and salt. Add flour mixture to sugar mixture and mix well. Roll ½-inch thick and spread filling over. Roll up and let sit overnight in refrigerator. Slice and bake on cookie sheet for 15 to 20 minutes.

Mix filling ingredients in large sauce pan and cook over medium low heat until thick.

Golden Pecan Tassies

1 cup butter, room temperature
6 ounces cream cheese, room temperature
2 cups flour, sifted

Filling
2 eggs
2 tablespoons butter, melted
1 ½ cups brown sugar, firmly packed
½ teaspoon vanilla
Dash of salt
1 cup pecans, whole

Heat oven to 350°. Blend butter, cream cheese and flour with hands into smooth dough. Shape into muffin or tart pans, making a shell. This amount should pat into three dozen medium tart or muffin tins. Fill with pecan filling and bake for 15 minutes. Reduce heat to 250° and bake 10 minutes more or until filling is firm.

For filling, beat eggs slightly and add butter, brown sugar, vanilla, and salt. Place just enough nuts to cover bottom of unbaked shells and fill three-quarters full of brown sugar mixture. These retain flaky melting goodness in freezer or foil.

Honey Cookies

3/4 cup shortening
1 cup sugar
1/4 cup honey
1 egg, beaten
1/4 teaspoon salt
1 ½ teaspoons cinnamon
1 ½ teaspoons baking soda
1 ½ teaspoons baking powder
1 ½ cups flour

Heat oven to 350°. Cream shortening and sugar. Add honey and beaten egg. Beat well. Sift dry ingredients together and add to sugar mixture. Roll into small balls and roll balls in sugar. Bake for 9 minutes.

Mincemeat Cookies (Afton Kay)

1 cup shortening
1 ½ cups brown sugar
2 eggs, well beaten
¼ cup molasses
2 tablespoons sweetened canned milk
2 tablespoons water
1 ¼ cup mincemeat
3 cups flour
½ teaspoon salt
4 teaspoons baking powder
2 cups rolled oats

Heat oven to 400°. Cream shortening and brown sugar. Add eggs, molasses, milk, water and mincemeat. Sift flour, measure and sift again with salt and baking powder. Add rolled oats, combine with shortening mixture. Mix well. Drop by teaspoons two inches apart, Bake 12 minutes on greased baking sheet.

Powdered Sugar Cookies

1 cup powdered sugar
1 cup granulated sugar, plus more for rolling cookies
1 cup butter
1 cup oil
2 eggs
1 teaspoon vanilla
4 cups plus 4 tablespoon flour
1 teaspoon baking soda
1 teaspoon cream of tartar

Heat oven to 375°. Cream together the sugars, butter, oil, eggs, and vanilla. Whisk dry ingredients together and add to sugar mixture. Roll into balls. Roll balls in sugar and flatten with glass. Bake on parchment lined cookie sheets for 10 to 12 minutes.

Apple Cake

Mom made this cake for all three of our weddings.

2 eggs
2 cups sugar
1 teaspoons vanilla
2 cups flour
2 teaspoons baking powder
1/8 teaspoon salt
2 teaspoons cinnamon
½ cup oil
4 cups yellow delicious apples, chopped
1 cup walnuts, chopped

Frosting
6 ounces cream cheese, softened
3 tablespoons butter, softened
1 teaspoon vanilla
1 ½ cups powdered sugar
Milk (optional)

Heat oven to 350°. Beat eggs, add sugar and cream well. Add vanilla. Sift together flour, baking powder, salt and cinnamon. Add alternately with oil to egg mixture. Stir in apples and nuts. Bake in a buttered 9-x13-inch pan for 1 hour. Cool completely before frosting.

Mix cream cheese and butter with vanilla. Add powdered sugar and mix until smooth and spreadable adding milk if necessary to thin to desired consistency.

Apple-Whiskey Cake

Mom's sister Corrine, lived in New Mexico for years. She visited her sister often and loved New Mexico. She subscribed to New Mexico Magazine and when she discovered this recipe, she made it often.

Packed with some of New Mexico's finest ingredients – apples, pecans, and whiskey – this cake actually originated from Melissa Clark, a New York Times food writer. It can be made at least a day ahead of gifting or serving. You can use any Bundt or tube pan to prepare the cake. Serves 12

½ cup candied crystallized ginger, chopped
¼ cup bourbon or rye whiskey, preferably New Mexican (divided use)
2 sticks unsalted butter, softened, plus more to grease pan
2 ½ cups all-purpose flour, plus more to dust pan
1 cup pecans
2 teaspoons baking powder
1 teaspoon baking soda
1 teaspoon ground canela (Mexican cinnamon) or other cinnamon
1 teaspoon ground nutmeg
1 teaspoon salt
1 cup sour cream
1 tablespoon pure vanilla extract
1 ¾ dark brown sugar
4 large eggs, at room temperature
1 pound tangy apples, such a Granny Smith, peeled, then coarsely grated on box grater or in food processor
½ cup granulated sugar

Mix together ginger and ¼ cup whiskey in small bowl and let stand at least 10 minutes.

Heat oven to 325°. Grease and flour standard-size 12-cup Bundt cake pan.

Toast pecans in small, heavy skillet over medium-low heat, stirring occasionally, until fragrant, about 4 minutes. When cool. Finely chop pecans.

Whisk together in bowl 2 ½ cups flour, baking powder, baking soda, canela, nutmeg, and salt.

In another bowl, whisk together sour cream and vanilla. Drain off whiskey from ginger into sour cream mixture and whisk again.

In stand mixer with paddle attachment, beat together 2 sticks butter and brown sugar on medium speed until light and fluffy, about 4 minutes. Stop and scrape down mixture as needed to combine well. Beat in eggs singly, mixing each in for about 30 seconds. Add flour and sour cream mixtures to mixer bowl in three stages each, alternating between mixtures. Remove bowl from mixer and fold in ginger, apples, and pecans. Batter will be thick.

Scrape batter into prepared pan. Bake about 70 minutes, until medium brown. A toothpick inserted in center of cake should come out clean.

Cool in pan 20 minutes, then run paring knife carefully around inside of pan. Invert on baking rack, remove pan, and let cool about 10 minutes more. Place cake on platter or cake stand. Make 20 slits around cake's surface with paring knife.

Stir together in small pan remaining ½ cup whiskey with granulated sugar. Warm over low heat and stir until sugar dissolves. Spoon whiskey mixture slowly all over still slightly warm cake. Let sit until room temperature. Serve, or cover cake to keep for up to one day. Once cut, it will remain flavorful for an additional couple of days.

Altitude adjustments: At 7,000 feet, reduce baking powder by ¼ teaspoon and baking soda by 1/8 teaspoon. Add 1 tablespoon of water to sour cream mixture. At about 5,000 feet, reduce baking powder by 1/8 teaspoon and baking soda by a big pinch. Add 1 ½ teaspoons water to sour cream mixture.

German's Sweet Chocolate Cake

1 4-oz. package German's sweet chocolate
½ cup boiling water
2 ½ cups sifted cake flour
1 teaspoon baking soda
½ teaspoon salt
1 cup butter
2 cups sugar
4 eggs, separated
1 teaspoon vanilla
1 cup buttermilk

Coconut-Pecan Frosting
1 cup evaporated milk
1 cup sugar
3 egg yolks, slightly beaten
½ cup butter
1 teaspoon vanilla
1 1/3 cup angel flake coconut
1 cup pecans, chopped

Heat oven to 350°. Melt chocolate in boiling water. Cool. In medium bowl sift flour with salt and baking soda. In large bowl cream butter and sugar until fluffy. Add egg yolks one at a time, beating well after each addition. Blend in vanilla and chocolate. Add flour and buttermilk alternately to chocolate mixture, beating after addition until smooth. Beat egg whites until stiff and fold into batter. Pour into three 8- or 9-inch layer cake pans. Bake for 30 to 40 minutes. Cool. Frost tops only with Coconut-Pecan Frosting.

Combine all ingredients except coconut and pecans in a medium sauce pan. Cook and stir over medium heat until thickened about twelve minutes. Add coconut and pecans. Cool until thick enough to spread. If frosting gets too hard to spread, beat it. Makes 2 ½ cups.

Pumpkin Cake Roll (Witt)

Mom was married to Witt for close to forty years. He brought this recipe into the marriage and we all loved it.

3 eggs
1 cup sugar
2/3 cup canned pumpkin
1 teaspoon lemon juice
¾ cup flour
1 teaspoon baking powder
½ teaspoon salt
2 teaspoons cinnamon
½ teaspoon nutmeg
1 teaspoon ginger
1 cup walnuts or pecans, chopped

Filling
6 ounces cream cheese, room temperature
4 tablespoons butter, room temperature
½ teaspoon vanilla
1 cup powdered sugar

Heat oven to 375°. Butter and flour a baking sheet. In a medium bowl, whisk flour, baking powder, salt, cinnamon, nutmeg, and ginger. In a large bowl, beat eggs and sugar with an electric mixer on high speed. Stir in pumpkin and lemon juice. Mix in dry ingredients. Pour into prepared pan and top with nuts. Bake 15 minutes. Using a flour sifter, sprinkle a dish towel the size of the cake pan with powdered sugar. Place the cake upside down on the dish towel and roll the cake. When cool, unroll and fill with filling.

Cream butter and cream cheese together with vanilla. Add powdered sugar. Spread filling over cooled cake. Roll cake again.

Texas Sheet Cake or Hot Fudge Cake Squares

2 cups flour
2 cups sugar
2 sticks butter
1 cup water
4 tablespoons cocoa
½ teaspoon cinnamon
2 eggs, lightly beaten
½ cup buttermilk
1 teaspoon baking soda
1 teaspoon vanilla

Marshmallow-Fudge Frosting
1 stick butter
6 tablespoons milk
4 tablespoons cocoa
1 cup mini-marshmallows
1 teaspoon vanilla
1 box powdered sugar
1 cup pecans, chopped

Heat oven to 350°. Mix flour and sugar in a large bowl. Place butter, water, cocoa, and cinnamon in pan and bring to a boil. Pour boiling mixture over flour and sugar and beat well. Stir baking soda into buttermilk and add that and eggs to flour and sugar mixture. Pour mixture into a greased baking sheet. Bake 15 to 20 minutes. While cake is baking, make marshmallow-fudge frosting.

For frosting, melt butter in large sauce pan. Add milk, cocoa and marshmallows and stir over low heat until marshmallows melt, and all ingredients are blended. Add vanilla and powdered sugar. Beat well. Add pecans and quickly spread over cake while cake and frosting are still hot. Allow to cool before cutting. Serves 20.

Cake Donuts (Irene Butler)

Irene was mom's father's sister. These donuts were legendary in our family.

4 cups flour
1 tablespoon butter
1 ½ cups sugar
1 ¾ teaspoon cream of tartar
2 ¼ teaspoon soda
1 teaspoon salt
1 teaspoon cinnamon
1 teaspoon nutmeg
2 eggs, beaten
 1 ½ cup buttermilk (or sour milk)

Work butter into flour. Add the rest of the dry ingredients and mix. Beat eggs and add buttermilk and beat together. Add to flour mixture. Mix on floured cloth and pat out to ½ inch thickness. Cut out and fry in deep fat. If mixture seems too soft mix a small amount of flour in but not too much. They will be hard to handle if too soft. Test donut hole in hot grease for right temperature. When frying donuts, you can prevent them from absorbing too much fat by adding a spoonful of vinegar to the hot fat.

Spudnuts (Janice Freeman)

Janice was mom's sister. She was two years older and died in March of 2022.

2 cups milk
1 ¼ cup sugar
Salt to taste
½ cup lard
1 cup mashed potatoes
3 eggs
½ teaspoon nutmeg
2 packages yeast
1/3 cup water
8-9 cups flour

Glaze
1 box powdered sugar
½ cup hot water
1 teaspoon vanilla

Scald milk, add sugar, salt, lard and potatoes. Cool to lukewarm. Mix eggs, nutmeg, yeast and water. Add milk mixture to egg mixture. Add enough flour to make a workable dough. Kneed and let rise until double. Punch down, divide and roll to ½ inch thickness. Cut and let rise until double. Fry at 350°. Drain and glaze. Makes 6-8 dozen.

Mix powdered sugar, hot water and vanilla together until smooth.

Banana Velvet Bread

½ cup butter
1 cup sugar
2 eggs, separated
3 ripe bananas, well mashed
1 teaspoon baking soda
2 tablespoons sour milk
2 cups flour
½ teaspoon salt
½ cup chopped walnuts

Heat oven to 350°. Cream butter and sugar. Add egg yolks, mashed bananas, and baking soda dissolved in the milk. Add dry ingredients and nuts. Blend well. Fold in stiffly beaten egg whites. Pour into buttered 8½" x 4½" x 2⅝" loaf pan and bake for 1 hour until toothpick inserted into center comes out clean.

Cinnamon Rolls

1 ½ cups cooled scalded milk
1 ½ cups water
6 tablespoons melted shortening
1 cup sugar
3 yeast cakes
3 eggs, beaten
1 teaspoon salt
8 cups flour
Melted butter
Cinnamon
Sugar

Combine scalded milk, water, shortening, sugar, yeast cakes, eggs and salt. Add flour. Mixture is very gooey. Let rise until double in bulk. Do not knead. Roll on floured board to ¾-inch thick. Spread with melted butter and sprinkle with cinnamon and sugar. Roll and cut. Raise until light 45 minutes to 1 hour. Bake in 375° oven for 12 minutes.

Sour Dough Cinnamon Rolls

Mom got on a sourdough kick at some point. She made all things sourdough from pancakes to bread to cinnamon rolls. The cinnamon rolls were the favorite of everyone, including her hair dresser, dog groomer, CPA and everyone else she shared them with.

Do not screw lid tightly on starter. Leave loose. It must breathe.

Step 1:
Add to starter (a.m.)
1 cup flour
½ cup sugar
1 cup warm water
3 heaping tablespoons instant potato flakes

Stir, leave uncovered at room temperature all day. Stir occasionally.

Step 2:
Remove 1 cup starter from bowl. Return rest of starter to the refrigerator. Save the left-over starter 3-7 days, then repeat Step 1.
Add to 1 cup starter:
1/3 cup sugar
1 ½ cup warm water
½ cup oil
1 tablespoon salt
1 package yeast
5 ½ cups flour

Mix together. Place dough in well buttered bowl. Turn to butter top. Cover. Let rise all night.

Step 3:
Place dough on floured board. Divide into 2 sections. Knead 8-10 times. Roll out each section into a 16 x 12-inch rectangle.

Make Cinnamon Sugar Filling

Using pastry brush, cover the entire surface of each rectangle
with melted butter. Mix brown sugar and cinnamon and sprinkle
half over each rectangle. Sprinkle half of the raisins onto each
rectangle. If you have people who do not like raisins, leave them
off one rectangle. Working with the long side, roll the dough into
a log pressing down as you go. With seam down, cut the log into
8 2-inch sections using an oiled knife or bench scraper. Place 8
rolls in each pan. Cover with buttered waxed paper. Let rise all
day.

Step 4: Bake at 375° for 18 to 22 minutes. Remove from oven
and let cool for 5 minutes before glazing. While the rolls are
baking, prepare the glaze.

Cinnamon Sugar Filling
½ cup butter, melted
2 cups brown sugar
4 tablespoons cinnamon
½ cup raisins

Glaze
1 cup confectioner's sugar
¼ teaspoon salt
3 tablespoons butter
1 teaspoon vanilla
2-4 tablespoons milk or heavy cream

Whisk confectioner's sugar and salt in medium bowl. Add butter
and vanilla. Stir in 2 tablespoons milk adding more as necessary
to make a smooth, spreadable glaze.

Brownies (Mildred McCarty)

Mildred was our dad's mom. She was never in the kitchen without an apron. She made these brownies often, giving them to us at Christmas in one of Granddad's King Edward cigar boxes. Yes, the egg in the frosting is raw. It never killed any of us so we're betting you'll be fine.

2/3 cup sifted flour
½ teaspoon salt
¾ teaspoon baking powder
2 eggs, well beaten
1 cup sugar
2 squares unsweetened chocolate
6 tablespoons butter
1 teaspoon vanilla
½ cup walnuts, chopped

Chocolate Deluxe Icing
2 cups sifted confectioner's sugar
1/3 teaspoon salt
1 large egg
1/3 cup butter or margarine, softened
2 squares Baker's bitter chocolate, melted and cooled slightly
1 teaspoon vanilla
16 whole walnuts

Heat oven to 350°. Grease and flour 8- or 9-inch square pan. Sift flour with salt and baking powder. Cream eggs and sugar. Melt together chocolate and butter, blend until smooth. Combine all mixtures and add vanilla and chopped nuts. They are done when they pull away from sides of pan and have a dull look on the top.

Beat all icing ingredients but walnuts until fluffy. Spread over brownies. Cut into 16 pieces and top each with a whole walnut.

Party Brownies

2 cups sugar
1 cup butter
2 teaspoons vanilla
4 eggs
1 ½ cups flour
1/3 cup cocoa
1 cup walnuts, chopped
1 package miniature marshmallows

Icing
1 stick butter
1/3 cup cream or milk
¼ cup cocoa
1 2/3 cups powdered sugar, sifted

Heat oven to 350°. Blend together sugar and butter. Add vanilla and eggs and mix well. Stir in flour and cocoa. Add walnuts. Pour into a 9-by 13-inch pan and bake for 45 minutes. Spread marshmallows over baked brownie mixture and return to oven until melted. Cool completely and ice.

Beat together butter, cream or milk, cocoa and powdered sugar with electric mixer until smooth.

Sex in a Pan!

Combine:
1 ½ cups flour
1 ½ sticks butter, room temperature
1 cup pecans, chopped

Heat oven to 350°. Press into bottom of 13 x 9 x 2-inch pan and bake 12-15 minutes until barely golden. Cool 20 minutes.

Beat together:
1 8-ounce package cream cheese, room temperature
1 cup powdered sugar

Fold in:
1 cup Cool Whip

Spread over baked crust.

Mix together:
3 boxes instant pudding, any flavor
3 cups milk

Spread over cream cheese mixture in pan. Top with remaining Cool Whip. Chill at least 2 hours.

Gimpie's Peanut Brittle (A.J. Freeman)

*A.J. was married to mom's sister, Janice. He shared this recipe
with Witt who makes this often for friends and family.*

2 cups sugar
1 cup water
1 cup light corn syrup
Dash of salt
2 tablespoons vanilla
1 stick butter
2 cups raw Spanish peanuts
1 ¼ tablespoon baking soda

Mix sugar, water, corn syrup, salt, vanilla, and butter in large fry
pan. Heat on medium heat (about #6 on electric stove). Bring to
a boil. Add Spanish peanuts. Stir often. Heat until small puffs of
smoke emerge from mixture. Sprinkle the baking soda over the
mixture. Turn heat off. Stir rapidly for 15 seconds. Pour into a
greased 11-inch by 17-inch baking sheet. Do not spread the
mixture. Let it spread on its own. Let cool completely. Remove
from pan. Break into pieces by hitting smooth side of brittle with
the bottom side of a large serving spoon. Put into sandwich bags.

Drink

Kahlua

It became a tradition to make this Kahlua in late October and bottle it after Thanksgiving. It is given as Christmas gifts to the special people in our lives.

2 ounces instant coffee
4 cups sugar
2 cups boiling water
1 pint brandy
1 vanilla bean

Mix and stir coffee, sugar, and water. Cool 2 hours. Add brandy and vanilla bean. Store in large bottle. Leave sealed for 30 days.

Wedding Mints

1 3 oz. package cream cheese
2 ½ cups powdered sugar
¼ teaspoon flavoring
Food coloring

Mix together and place in mint molds. Refrigerate until firm.
Remove from molds and store in refrigerator in airtight container.

About the Author

Liz McCarty is a chef extraordinaire. She has worked with some of the world's most famous chefs. She has attended cooking schools in San Francisco, San Diego, Phoenix, New Orleans, Mexico, Italy, Puerto Rico, and fileted tuna in the Tokyo fish market. Is it any wonder that she was intrigued with the idea of putting together a book of recipes?

Liz's father, Jim McCarty, instilled in her and her sisters a strong sense of "family". When the recipes came from her mother, there was no choice. Liz had to create this book.

Before retiring to the "good life", Liz spent twenty-five years building a successful real estate company with offices in four Arizona cities. After selling her company, she prepared to "sail away" on the high seas with her husband Howard Jones. She has lived in the mountains of Arizona, in an ocean-view home in San Diego, and in Mexico. She now calls Scottsdale, Arizona home base.

She plays the flute. She has climbed Mount Kilimanjaro. She has served on the boards of major companies, public health facilities, and charitable organizations. She has been around the world and she has held The Stanley Cup. She has a wonderful daughter and four grandchildren. She believes life is to be lived and she's doing her best to live it.

h. Alton Jones – June 2024

www.ingramcontent.com/pod-product-compliance
Lightning Source LLC
Chambersburg PA
CBHW051212090426
42742CB00021B/3427